the **Beatles**
Way

the **Beatles Way**

FAB WISDOM FOR EVERYDAY LIFE

Larry Lange

BEYOND
WORDS
Publishing
I N C

Beyond Words Publishing, Inc.
20827 N.W. Cornell Road, Suite 500
Hillsboro, Oregon 97124-9808
503-531-8700
1-800-284-9673

Editor: Laura Carlsmith
Managing editor: Julie Steigerwaldt
Proofreader: Marvin Moore
Design: Big-Giant
Cover photograph: Apple Corps/Camera Press/Retna
Composition: William H. Brunson Typography Services

Printed in the United States of America
Distributed to the book trade by Publishers Group West

Library of Congress Cataloging-in-Publication Data
Lange, Larry.
    The Beatles way : fab wisdom for everyday life / Larry Lange.
        p.   cm.
    Includes bibliographical references.
    ISBN 1-58270-061-3 (pbk.)
    1. Conduct of life.   2. Beatles—Miscellanea.   I. Title.

    BF637.C5 L36   2001
    158.1—dc21

                                                        2001037451

The corporate mission of Beyond Words Publishing, Inc.:
Inspire to Integrity

For Josh and Naomi.
You are the halves
of my heart.

CONTENTS

Introduction   ix

1 Dream   2

2 Goals   20

3 Attitude   46

4 Team   70

5 Control   96

6 Evolve   124

7 Spirit   150

Afterword   163

Acknowledgments   167

Bibliography   169

The Beatles way of life
was like a young kid entering the big world,
entering it with friends and conquering it totally.
And that was fantastic. An incredible experience.

—Paul McCartney

The Beatles as personal-growth gurus? I say unequivocally, *"Yeah! Yeah! Yeah!"*

Certainly, the music of the Beatles means so much to so many around the world, even thirty years after the group disbanded. But let's take a closer look at the full Beatle success phenomenon—and how it can directly benefit you, your dreams, your work, your family, and your search for personal fulfillment, inner peace, and sheer unadulterated joy.

If ever four people adhered adamantly to the success—and self-help—principles espoused by Anthony Robbins, Stephen Covey, Wayne Dyer, Marianne Williamson, or Deepak Chopra, they would surely be those world-renowned lads from Liverpool—John Lennon, Paul McCartney, George Harrison, and Ringo Starr.

Though all four Beatles have stated they never *consciously* practiced any formal goal-setting plan during their rocket-ride to success, by making a study of their well-documented rise, we can piece together how the Beatles did achieve their wildest, and even their most unanticipated, unimaginable dreams. And in this book, you'll see how their wisdom can be distilled into seven clear, precise, and understandable principles that you can use in your life. And you'll learn how to *consciously* incorporate these principles into your own life, enabling you, like the Beatles, to manifest your dreams into exciting realities.

The Seven Fab Wisdom Principles
"In My Life"
(*Rubber Soul*, 1965)

As a Beatlemaniac, I've been around long enough to have seen the Beatles perform on *The Ed Sullivan Show* in 1964, but I am still young enough to be thrilled when "She Loves You" leaps off the radio even today. Additionally, I've had Beatlesque experience as a songwriter for a major music publisher as well as several years as a journalist covering the successes and failures of corporations on the bleeding-edge of technology. This triple perspective of fan, colleague, and critic gives me a unique vantage point in translating the Beatles' success principles into a practical and user-friendly format.

I call these seven wisdom principles *fab* because the Beatles were known around the world as the "Fab Four." They created something even more important than an incredible legacy of music and film—a model of freedom from inhibition and convention, a freedom defined by one simple Liverpudlian word: fab!

The Beatles Way is being creative, original, elegant, intelligent, fearless, humorous, daring, inventive, relevant, versatile, accessible, and honest as well as staying focused on your unique and worthwhile dreams.

If you're looking to start a small business, realize a personal dream, or perhaps even point your children toward a challenging and creative lifestyle, the fab wisdom of the Beatles will clearly light your way.

The Beatles Way shows how to live the life you've been dreaming of. Or if you simply desire to add more joy, more peace, or even more fun into your daily routine, this book has the answers.

This book is packed with anecdotes and little-known quotes from the Beatles and those in their inner circle. These principles highlight the major thought-processes of the Beatles from their ragged beginnings as a rough-and-tumble beat group, through their time as unofficial world princes, to their canonization as cultural icons.

The Impact of the Beatles on the World
"The act you've known for all these years..."
("Sgt. Pepper's Lonely Hearts Club Band," 1967)

To set the stage, let's take a look at just how big an impact the Beatles have had on our lives and how they continue to affect us today. Take a look at some of these statistics of the Beatles' legacy:

★ The Beatles have sold over *one billion* records worldwide.

★ Their CD, *1*, a compilation of the group's biggest hits, is expected to become the biggest-selling recording in history. In the weeks after its 2000 release, it was number one on the charts in thirty countries.

★ Thirty years after the Beatles disbanded, the finance magazine *Forbes* placed the group third in its annual table of entertainment profit-makers, behind only movie and sports moguls Tom Cruise and Tiger Woods.

★ The television series *Anthology*, which aired in 1995 (twenty-five years after the group broke up) was seen by 420 million people in ninety-four countries. The first double-CD in the *Anthology* series sold 8.9 million copies in the first seven weeks, landing the Number One spot in *Billboard* magazine.

★ In Australia, 300,000 fans turned out to see the Beatles in Adelaide during one day in July 1964. Thirty-six years later, they're still drawing the crowds: in the summer of 2000, the city of Liverpool hosted

350,000 fans from around the world for its annual Beatles celebration, and the city receives over 500,000 Beatles fans each year who visit the Fab Four's haunts.

★ The Beatles won fourteen Grammy Awards with over thirty nominations.

★ They earned one Academy Award and were nominated for two others.

Other lesser-known achievements include these:

★ The Beatles single-handedly brought the rock concert tour industry to new, international heights by performing at sports stadiums and touring worldwide.

★ The group was the first to deploy the music-video format as a promotional tool, now the de facto music-industry standard popularized by MTV.

★ The Beatles altered the nature of international recordings; until they came along, many big hit songs had to be translated before they would get foreign airplay. The conventional wisdom was that audiences would not listen to songs in a foreign language. The Beatles refused to re-record their songs, knowing they were perfect as originally recorded. The upshot of their self-confidence is that today, songs recorded in one language are heard all over the world in their original language.

★ The Beatles changed their image and music frequently and dramatically, risking critical and commercial failure while building ever-richer critical and popular successes for their entire career.

★ The Fab Four played live to a worldwide audience of 400 million via satellite during one single concert in 1967. This broadcast is also considered the first major high-tech linkup ever accomplished.

★ The Beatles expanded Western consciousness of the value of Eastern religion, including Zen Buddhism, Taoism, and Hinduism.

Whew! That's quite a list of heady achievements! While your own dreams might not include having such a global impact, the Beatles' legacy surely shows that virtually *anything* is possible. *Anything.*

What to Expect from This Book
"Roll up for the Mystery Tour..."
("Magical Mystery Tour," 1968)

So, are you interested in how these four scruffs from a gritty working-class city managed to turn the world upside down and make every one of their dreams come true? And are you keen on learning how you can do the same? Well, read on! Here's a quick overview of what to expect in the pages of *The Beatles Way.* Each of the seven chapters takes you on a light-hearted and informative look at how you can adopt the seven tenets of fab wisdom into your life.

1. *Dream* focuses on the power of dreaming. You'll see its positive effect on the Beatles and learn how a simple technique such as writing down or drawing out your dreams can be a catalyst for realizing them. You'll also discover how to develop passion for learning that doesn't necessarily require formal schooling or training.

2. *Goals* centers on how you, like the Beatles, can set and meet your goals with a methodical "staircase climb." You'll learn the importance of being superbly prepared, of deciding to do "whatever it takes" in order to reach your goals, and how to achieve them at a rapid rate.

3. *Attitude* highlights the fab tenet that underlies all else: *Attitude is everything.* You'll learn how to deal confidently with the unknown as you pursue your dreams. You'll find out how the Beatles handled intense pressure and harrowing fear while still daring to take risks and accomplish the hard work required of their dreams. You'll also learn

how the group's so-called "arrogance" worked to their benefit, as they rejected rejection, expected success, and kept themselves buoyed with humor.

4. *Team* features how important it is to create—and continually inspire— a loyal team. You'll learn how to work closely with your team toward mutual goals and a collective dream. You'll also discover how—as the Beatles did—to make tough sacrifices to further the team dream. This chapter also focuses on the importance of leadership and how the Beatles—and their team—rallied for two leaders—John and Paul—at critical points of time in their career.

5. *Control* teaches the importance of DIY (doing it yourself) and why it's important to keep tabs on all aspects of your dreams as they begin to manifest themselves. You'll be inspired when you read of how the Beatles trusted their instincts and maintained control over the creation and development of their image and projects while staying true to themselves.

6. *Evolve* shows you how to keep your dreams fresh and ever-evolving, just as the Beatles did throughout their career. You'll see that the realization of your dreams corresponds to your willingness to be outrageous, progressive, and adaptable as well as to your ability to work efficiently despite massive limitations. You'll look at the importance of being a leader whether at work, as a parent, or as a friend. You'll also learn, as the Beatles knew, that there is no such thing as a "mistake." This ability to evolve, lead, and even thrive is what can set you apart even during the worst times of crisis.

7. *Spirit* will show you how to foster within yourself an open-mindedness toward spirituality and social responsibility. As the Beatles did, you'll see how this freeing principle can enhance not only your life but the lives of everyone around you and can quite possibly even change the entire world for the better.

How to Use This Book

"There's nothing you can do that can't be done . . ."
("All You Need Is Love," 1968)

Although the seven tenets of fab wisdom in *The Beatles Way* are arranged to build on each other, they can be read in any order. Turn to any page and you'll glean unique Beatle wisdom that can guide you along in your own journey of success and personal fulfillment.

In each of the seven principles is a series of subtopics named with a related lyric or title from a Beatle song. As you read, let the powerful Beatle sentiments soak into your subconscious. Let them trigger your imagination and inspire you to act on your dreams.

At the end of each chapter, a section entitled "You're the Fifth Beatle!" offers exercises you can do anytime and anywhere to aid you in activating the fab wisdom into your own life.

OK, I'm just as excited as you are to get on with the "really big shew!" as Ed Sullivan would say, but permit me one last thought. The elegance of the Beatles' vision, along with their fiery energy, determination, and skill, stand as a testament and practical role model for you as you seek to live a profound, successful, and joyous life.

I sincerely hope the principles in this book provide *you* with all the wonder, excitement, and reward of *The Beatles Way*!

1 DREAM

I believe in everything

until it's disproved. So I believe in fairies, the myths, dragons.
It all exists —even if it's in your mind.
Who's to say that dreams and nightmares aren't as real as the here and now?
Reality leaves a lot to the imagination.

—John Lennon

To enjoy even a modicum of the success the Beatles achieved, the very first and most integral step you have to take is deceptively simple: *dream*.

Why "deceptively"? Well, in our hyper-efficient world where the ability to multitask is coveted and rewarded, it's not so easy to feel good about dreaming. When was the last time you took ten minutes—no, wait, *five* minutes—to dream, fantasize, or visualize your most fulfilling goals?

For John and his friend Paul McCartney, big dreams were the way out of the doldrums of rain-soaked Liverpool. "If I had been asked at fifteen why I wrote songs," Paul said, "I would have answered, 'money.' But after a while, you realize that's not really your driving motive. When you get the money, you still need to keep going ... there has to be something else. I think it's the freedom to *live your dreams*."

John discussed the impact of Elvis Presley on the Beatles' dreams and how dreams of Elvis-style success motivated the young group into action. Asked in 1971 what he was dreaming about as a kid in the late '50s, John instantly replied, "To be bigger than Elvis!" That was a pretty heady fantasy for an admitted rebel whose only profession was cutting class and picking fights.

"You went to see those Elvis movies when we were still in Liverpool, and you'd see everybody waiting there to see him.... I'd be waiting there too. And they'd all scream when he came on the screen," John said. Fellow dreamer George Harrison noted near-identical dreams at the time: "We looked at Buddy Holly and Elvis and thought, 'That looks like a good job ... money, travel, chicks, nice threads—there's a great deal to be said about playing rock 'n' roll!'" Maybe George's dreams weren't the loftiest, but hey, he was just a kid! As he matured, his dreams certainly evolved far beyond this search for material pleasures.

Choose Your Dreams: Choose Your Future

"And it's my mind, and there's no time..."
("There's a Place," 1963)

Look at the innermost thoughts of the Beatles through the most revealing of sources—their lyrics. You'll find proof that they consciously cultivated their dreams. "There's a Place," for instance, shows that John's earliest songwriting themes were based on a kind of meditative state: "There's a place where I can go ... And it's my mind, and there's no time..."

The lyrics are so simple yet profound. In your dreams, there is no time, there are no distractions, just the pureness of envisioning yourself however you want to be. If you believe, like the Beatles did, that your dreams are the starting point for your reality, let your mind wander right now down the path toward your future goal.

Only a mile away, like-minded rock 'n' roll enthusiast Paul McCartney was dreaming his young life away as well, and not in the sense of wasting time either. One of the first songs Paul wrote is "Like Dreamers Do," which reveals his secret of success in getting the girl—a confidence that what he dreams *will* happen. "I saw a girl in my dreams, / And so it seems / That I will love her."

Pretty insightful stuff from the fledgling young songwriters. At first glance, the simple act of dreaming might seem an obvious step in your success journey. But ask yourself, when was the last time you really gave yourself a break from your day's frantic activities to simply *daydream*?

Many motivational and spiritual teachers espouse dreaming as an effective tool in creating a more successful and joyous life. Shakti Gawain's *Creative Visualization* was a landmark book that has helped many to focus on this one step alone. For the business world, Anthony Robbins's best-selling books *Unlimited Power* and *Awaken the Giant Within* feature the dreaming process as a critical method in thwarting fear and self-destructive tendencies.

When asked about his secret to success, George quoted one of his spiritual muses, Mahatma Gandhi: "Create and preserve the image of your choice."

As for the last member to join the group, a twelve-year-old Ringo Starr would walk endlessly about the bleak Liverpool streets, peering into music-shop windows, visualizing the day he would have his own set of Ludwig drums. He said, "Drums were the only things I wanted. I used to look in shops and see the drums—I never looked at guitars." Ringo's dream strategy was to dream realistically—one obtainable goal at a time. When he got those drums, did he stop dreaming? Obviously not! Don't ever let yourself stop dreaming either. Your dreams are your first step to your next realities.

How's this for turning daydreams into realities? The Beatles, through the twin forces of their dreams and hard work, met, performed with, and befriended virtually every musical hero they ever dreamed about. In 1963, they toured with mentors Little Richard and Roy Orbison; a year later another one of their heroes, Carl Perkins, attended their recording session of his song "Matchbox," and they'd also met privately with Bob Dylan. And in 1965, they were slumming with Elvis Presley in his Bel-Air home, jamming, talking shop, and soaking in the manifestations of making the simple but oft-ignored choice to *dream*.

What about you—are you feeling inspired to take some time to *dream*?

Draw Your Dreams
"Picture yourself in a boat on a river..."
("Lucy in the Sky with Diamonds," 1967)

Another aspect of Beatle wisdom is straight out of the self-motivation wisdom of Napoleon Hill and Anthony Robbins: just take out pen, pencil, or even a box of crayons, and actually begin to *draw* your dreams down on paper. It's in the art of doing, say these teachers, that the dream actually becomes more and more tangible and exponentially easier to manifest as a reality.

Early on, a teenage Paul sketched out various Beatle logos and designed stage clothes for the band, including the shiny blue mohair suit adopted by the Beatles on their 1964 American tour—with even a hint of the soon-to-be-famous black-velvet collar.

George Harrison applied this technique as a perennially bored kid in school. "When I was thirteen or fourteen," said George, "I used to be at the back of the class drawing guitars—big cello cutaway guitars with 'f' holes [popular among blues players], little solid ones with pointed cutaways, and rounded cutaways. I was *totally* into guitars."

And Paul added that setting their dreams was critical in manifesting Beatle dreams into reality: "[John and I] would sit down with a school notebook—which I have to this day, an old tattered copybook—and I would write down anything we came up with, starting on the top of the first page with 'A Lennon/McCartney Original.' All the pages have got that. We saw ourselves as very much the next great songwriting team. Which, funnily enough, is what we became!" *Indeed*.

Now picture yourself in a boat on a river. Or earning $100,000 a year. Or finding time to spend a day a week volunteering at the homeless shelter. Now draw it. So, what if you're no Matisse or O'Keeffe? It's not the quality of the art you produce that matters—it's simply the fact that you're producing it: you're sketching out a picture of you, succeeding at your dream. This dream's for you and your eyes alone. First it's in your head, then it's on the paper, and then it's part of your daily life. Just like the Fab Four! *Yeah! Yeah! Yeah!*

Searching Your Subconscious
"Listen to the color of your dreams..."
("Tomorrow Never Knows," 1966)

Your unconscious dreams, the ones that come when you're asleep, half-awake, or daydreaming, should never be dismissed. Because your editorial, naysaying mind is off-duty at those times, these dreams may be the times of your greatest creativity.

John agreed, noting that it is in the periods of near-sleep where creation effectively takes place: "It's always in the middle of the night when you're half-awake, or [when you're] tired and your critical faculties are switched off."

Paul relayed a similar story concerning his own haunting composition "Let It Be": "One night during this tense time [in 1969 when the Beatles were breaking up], I had a dream that I saw my mother, who'd died ten years ago. It was so wonderful for me, and she was very reassuring. In the dream she said, 'It'll be alright.' I'm not sure if she said the words 'let it be,' but it was such a sweet dream, I woke up thinking, 'Oh it was really great to visit with her again.' I started the song off with 'Mother Mary,' which was her name."

For "Yellow Submarine," Paul remembered, "I was laying in bed, and there's a nice twilight zone just as you're drifting into sleep and as you wake from it, I always find it quite a comfortable zone. I remember think-ing that a children's song would be quite a good idea.... I was thinking of it as a song for Ringo, which it eventually turned out to be."

John commented on one of his most famous songs, "Strawberry Fields Forever," noting, "That's a real place—but I used it as an image. I was always seeing things in a hallucinatory way. Surrealism had a great effect on me, because I realized that the imagery in my mind wasn't insanity; that if I was insane, I belong in an exclusive club that sees the world in those terms. Surrealism to me is reality. Psychic vision to me is reality."

And finally, perhaps the most celebrated song in the Beatles canon was literally dreamed into existence. Listen to Paul as he describes the writing of "Yesterday": "I woke up with a lovely tune in my head. I thought, 'That's great—what is it?'" Paul stumbled over to the upright piano next to his bed and immediately found the chords to the tune. "I like the melody a lot," he continues, "but because I'd dreamed it, I couldn't believe I'd written it." Today, his song "Yesterday" stands as the most-broadcast—and most-covered—song of all time. It has been played over six million times on American radio alone. It would take over twenty-three years to play the song that many times nonstop.

How do you know the difference between a dream that's pointing you toward your future and one that's totally inexplicable and, likely, irrelevant to your goal? As Paul put it, there's a special feeling you get when you've opened yourself up to your dream-self and are rewarded: "It's that creative moment when you come up with an idea that's the greatest. You're filled with a knowledge that you're right, which, when much of your life is filled with guilt and the knowledge that you're prob-ably not right, is a magic moment.... It's a very warm feeling that comes all over you, and for some reason it comes from the spine, through the cranium, and out the mouth." Perhaps Paul didn't know it at the time, but he's discussing what Hinduism calls "awakening the kundalini," or arousing the inner energy during a moment of epiphany.

Sometimes, just as the Beatles did, you have to face the fact that dreams do end. But really, what's the end of one dream but the start of another? As John said in 1970 in his first solo album, *God*, after the Beatles broke up, "The dream is over, what can I say... And so dear friends, you'll just have to carry on / The dream is over."

So listen to what your dreams are saying. They may be the wisest part of you, trying to get past the whirlwind of your "responsible" mind. Go ahead, lie down on that couch and start dreaming!

Learn What You Love

"It's gotta be rock 'n' roll music..."
("Rock and Roll Music," 1964)

OK, you're in agreement—dreaming is a big factor in achieving success. So, what's next? We've seen that drawing or writing the dream can lead to its fruition, but the next natural step in actually doing something about your dreams is—are you ready for a little hard work?—*learning*. Even if you're a genius like Lennon and McCartney, you still have to work hard at your passion—and if you're not a genius, so what? As one of the Beatles' biggest influences, Brian Wilson, said during his halcyon days as writer, producer, and performer for the Beach Boys, "I'm not a genius—I'm just a hard workin' guy."

For you, learning to master the intricacies of your chosen profession or avocation could become a constant driving factor bordering on obsession. You'll be in good company.

Paul's brother Mike—himself a respected British musician and comedian—said, "The minute Paul got his guitar [at age fourteen], that was the

end—he was lost. He didn't have time to eat or drink or think about anything else. He played it on the lavatory, in the bath, everywhere."

The Beatles consumed the records of their rock 'n' roll and R&B
heroes—Chuck Berry, Jerry Lee Lewis, Gene Vincent, Fats Domino, and
New Orleans rock 'n' roller Larry Williams—studying their arrangements
and production values. They learned to echo the vocal stylings of Eddie
Cochran, the Everly Brothers, the Isley Brothers, and Little Richard. In
fact, when the two met later, Little Richard actually helped Paul refine his
high "woo!" vocal technique.

The Beatles treated their musical heroes as their virtual teachers, and
their textbooks were albums and 45s. As each batch of new records came
off the boats at the Liverpool docks, Ringo noted, "You'd kill for that bit
of plastic." The lesson for you: Obsession can be good!

Concurrently, John and Paul were writing dozens of original compositions between 1956 and 1962; some estimates, including Paul's, put the
number at one hundred. By the time they were under a recording contract, as George Harrison has said, the two had "written out" most of their
bad songs. Paul talks about those early songwriting days: "John and I
used to sag off school and play hooky. We'd go to my house and try to
learn to play songs. He had these banjo chords, and I'd have half a guitar
chord. We started from the same place and then went on the same railway
journey together."

In their insatiable appetite to learn, Paul said, "We literally went across
town for one chord, the B7th. We all knew E and A, but the last one of the
sequence is B7, and it's a very tricky one. But there was a guy that knew it,
so we all got on the bus and went to his house." He added that he and his fellow Beatles also journeyed across town to find a record, "Searchin'," by the
Coasters. "We had to get on the bus . . . do two changes of bus routes. Didn't
matter—there was a passion about that song." He added insightfully, "I think
that dedication is what separated the Beatles from a lot of other bands."

It's your dedication to your job, to your family, to your passion, that separates *you* from others who are doing the same thing.

All the Beatles were literature buffs as well, which gave them another dimension to draw their music from. John's passion for Lewis Carroll's *Alice in Wonderland* became the inspiration for many of his psychedelic-style lyrical works during his *Sgt. Pepper* and *Magical Mystery Tour* period. And Paul, who was quite familiar with Shakespeare, he noted how he "followed the Bard" and ended the "Act" of side two of the *Abbey Road* album with a "meaningful Shakespeare-style couplet"—his song "The End."

Paul was raised on jazz; his dad was an amateur jazz musician. Accustomed to grooving at home to Glenn Miller pieces like "In the Mood" and brassy big-band numbers, these influences soon found their way into Paul's own work. "Can't Buy Me Love" was the first full-blown "swing" song by Paul, and during the *Revolver* and *Sgt. Pepper* albums, almost every song of his was set in a "swing" time signature of 12/8.

George Martin, the Beatles' longtime record producer, said, "The turning point [for the group's maturation as artists] was 'Can't Buy Me Love.'" He added, "I don't know how to explain what makes a song sophisticated. But I know that song is, because, about two years after the Beatles did it, I recorded a cover version of it with Ella Fitzgerald, and boy, it suited her. She loved it and she swung like mad. That shows you the sophistication of that song."

In his quenchless thirst for learning, Paul veered far from his jazz roots, studying a wide variety of music from Broadway show tunes to ballroom dance numbers from the '30s and '40s. Likewise, John's mother, Julia, taught her son old-time banjo favorites as well as numbers from the Disney catalog. Intellectual though he was, John could still lay down a mean "When You Wish upon a Star"! It's all fodder for genius.

For both Beatles, this kind of diverse learning figured predominantly in the group's ability to write and perform virtually any style of music—

from sentimental ballads, to Fred Astaire–type tunes, to comedy-folk songs, to the most raucous rock 'n' roll.

So, once you've found your passion, do as the Beatles did: Explore every permutation, every facet of your field of interest, whether it's baking bread, selling on-line merchandise, or raising children.

And in your field, get specific with your goals, whether it's to bake the best brioche in town or to sell the most e-books in the country or to be the best parent to your toddler son. Temper some of your diverse learning with the down-and-dirty how-to's: Study people who are the best, glean what it is that makes them the best, and then apply—don't call it copying!—their tactics to your life.

That's what the young Beatles did. Besides immersing themselves in the music of their heroes, they also were students of the specific tactics of legendary songwriters such as Buddy Holly, Bob Dylan, and the Beach Boys' leader Brian Wilson along with the great songwriting teams such as Leiber and Stoller (Elvis Presley's writers) and Gerry Goffin and Carole King (songwriters of "Up on the Roof," "The Loco-Motion," and "Will You Still Love Me Tomorrow"). The group also learned to harmonize from their Motown mentors Smokey Robinson and the Miracles, the Marvelettes, and the Ronettes.

The Beatles weren't above having heroes. They didn't start out cockily thinking they could accomplish their dreams on their own. And they didn't worry about copping some bits from their heroes. They were wise to emulate the best and to use what they learned as a springboard to their own unique take on rock 'n' roll. Paul said that when he and John discovered Elvis Presley as teenagers, the reaction was immediate: "That's it. That is the guru we have been waiting for—the Messiah has *arrived*!" And that's the message: Don't reinvent the wheel in an effort to be "original and authentic." Find your heroes, borrow from them, and your own style will flow naturally from all that you've learned.

Dare to Be Experimental

"I didn't know what I would find there..."
("Got to Get You into My Life," 1966)

Once you've gotten the basics down, from studying all you can about your passion and emulating the best of the best, it's time to experiment! Have fun! The Beatles, even early on, pushed hard against stodgy music-industry boundaries. All of the Beatles had long-standing interests in classical and avant-garde music. This background stood them in good stead during their experimental days. John's interest in early '60s French experimental music, which included an element of a repetitive musical phrase, proved useful when "I Want to Hold Your Hand" needed an introduction. Remembering his French influences, he grabbed the chord sequence from the middle section ("I can't hide, I can't hide, I can't hiiiiide!") and put it at the beginning as well, which provided the song with its unique explosive kickoff.

And it's little known that Beethoven's "Moonlight" Sonata, with the chords played backwards, is the musical theme of John's *Abbey Road* song "Because." Not your standard musical technique back in the 1960s! Additionally, the Beatles signed to their personal label Apple Records one of the most innovative modern classical composers, John Tavener. And a prime example of how *not* to stand still and atrophy is Paul. He has evolved far from his rhythm and blues and jazz roots and is today a respected classical composer, a direction he began heading toward in the mid-1990s—when he was in his fifties. Paul also records groundbreaking ambient music today—his experimental *Liverpool Sound Collage* album was nominated for a Grammy in 2001.

Obviously, there was nothing off-limits for the Beatles musically, and this probably more than anything was a factor in their ongoing ability to develop as artists. It's true for you too. Keep learning, keep trying new things, don't stop changing—it's as true for artists as it is for doctors, parents, gardeners, salespeople, or politicians. Like the Beatles, never let yourself become stagnant in one style, no matter how much success that style has brought you.

Formal Education Not Required

"Don't wanna go to school to learn to read 'n' write..."
("Bad Boy," 1964)

Now it's time to speak of the flip side of learning: side B, the "fake it till you make it" philosophy. It's easy to stay in learner mode, collecting information and dreaming of hypothetical successes. But sometimes it's better to just jump in, ready or not! That too was the Beatles way.

None of the Beatles, despite their passion for learning, had formal musical training. All four are self-taught—and proud of it. Paul never learned to read music and talks openly about how he consciously avoids learning what the "little black squigglies" (music notation) represent, as it would only hamper his creativity.

Here's John on the subject in 1966: "When it started with me and George, Paul, and Ringo, we said, 'Listen, man!' This is a field of professionalism that doesn't need any qualifications, except that you've got to get down to it, and want to do it, and you can make it without a college education." John drives the point home about vocal prowess: "I didn't have to be trained as a singer. I can sing. Singing is singing to people who enjoy what you're singing, not being able to hold a note."

Ringo too is blunt on this point. Forty years before Nike's famous slogan, he knew how important it is sometimes to "Just do it": "I didn't study drums. I joined hands and made all the mistakes onstage." He added, "I feel I learn more from professionals, rather than from going to school. I don't particularly want to go to a class, when I can get on with someone who knows his gig and who can teach me."

And even after learning it would take years of study to play the sitar properly, George wasn't deterred. His mentor and sitar master, Ravi Shankar, said in 1968, "Tapping into his own knowledge of the guitar, [George] experimented on his own, but he always expressed the desire to learn to play it properly." While he was still years away from being a master, George's sitar stylings on "Norwegian Wood" in 1965 are evidence that total mastery is not a prerequisite for beauty or success.

The point to it all is, don't be intimidated by "the way things have always been done." If you're good, or even if you're just on your way to being good, don't stay in the cosseted walls of academia or novice-hood too long. Be fab! Be daring! Just do it!

Inspiration All Around You

"In my ears and in my eyes . . ."
("Penny Lane," 1967)

Just as you don't have to go to church to be inspired, you don't always have to go to school to learn. The Beatles drew inspiration from their world as it happened to be, each day of their lives: their childhood, co-workers, friends, lovers, relatives—in short, to paraphrase "Penny Lane," from the sights and sounds "in their ears and in their eyes." In fact, Penny Lane is a real district in Liverpool, and the barbershop mentioned in the song is where pre-teens John, George, and Paul received monthly haircuts.

One of John's favorite childhood places and the title of one of his songs is Strawberry Field, an old Victorian manor. It was adjacent to his Aunt Mimi's house where he lived, and there he would often play—and dream—in this secret garden hideaway.

The Beatles are master teachers of refining the most mundane events in life into the sublime: If Paul got a parking ticket, he immediately sat down at the piano and worked up a song around the bobby who wrote him up. "Lovely Rita" was inspired by London traffic warden Meta Davies. Likewise, "Magical Mystery Tour" is an actual holiday event for day-trippers in England. "[There was a holiday] called a 'Mystery Tour' up north in England," said Paul. "When we were kids, you'd get on a bus and didn't know where you were going."

John's two *Sgt. Pepper* classics "Lucy in the Sky with Diamonds" and "Being for the Benefit of Mr. Kite!" were derived from two ordinary occurrences in his life—his four-year-old son Julian's pastel painting and a poster from an antique store, respectively. The famed "Lucy" was actually Julian's school-chum Lucy O'Donnell, and the authentic antique circus poster he had acquired during the *Pepper* sessions reveals that the words to "Mr. Kite" were gleaned from it practically word-for-word.

One of John's most awe-inspiring songs, "A Day in the Life," was prompted by a bit in a newspaper. John said, "I was writing the song with the *Daily Mail* propped up in front of me on the piano. I had it open to the 'News In Brief' and there was a paragraph about four thousand holes being discovered in Blackburn, Lancashire."

George too took inspiration from his daily activities. "While My Guitar Gently Weeps" came to him at the time he was being heavily influenced by the *I Ching: The Book of Changes*, which features the Eastern spiritual concept that everything is relative to everything else, as opposed to the Western view that things are merely coincidental or random. "The idea was in my head," said George, "so I decided to write a song based on the first thing I saw upon opening any book, as it would be relative to that moment." He added, "I picked up a book at random, opened it, and saw 'gently weeps.' I then laid the book down again and started the song."

Two *White Album* classics by Paul also followed this methodology. "Ob-La-Di, Ob-La-Da" was inspired by "a fellow who used to hang around the clubs who used to say, [Jamaican accent] 'ob-la-di, ob-la-da, life goes on!' He was one of those guys who had great expressions." And

"Martha My Dear" began as a melody Paul played for his pet sheepdog of the same name.

For "Golden Slumbers," Paul related this story from 1969: "I was just playing the piano in Liverpool at my dad's house, and my sister Ruth's piano book was up on the stand. I was just flipping through it and I came to 'Golden Slumbers.' I can't read music, so I didn't know the tune, so I just started playing my tune to it. It just happened because I was reading her book."

From the Beatles' point of view, go ahead and soak in all the lessons from the masters who inspire you, but don't close your eyes to the ordinary world and the ordinary people all around you. Stay tuned to the fantastic ideas all around you, all the time, just waiting to be plucked from the creative vine.

YOU'RE THE FIFTH BEATLE! — *Dream*

The "Fifth Beatle" is an unofficial and fond term for some of the major contributors to the group's success. These include manager Brian Epstein, road manager and friend Neil Aspinall, record producer George Martin, and even self-proclaimed "Fifth Beatle" Murray "the K" Kaufman, the New York City–based disc jockey who helped launch the Fabs' career in the United States.

Now, here's your chance to join, at least in spirit, these illustrious "Fifth Beatle" alumni! Give these simple exercises a try. They reflect the techniques discussed in this chapter and will help you adopt the fab wisdom principles into your own life—the spirit that encourages your dreaming and excites you to the possibilities in life. You should begin seeing results right away. Why not? The effectiveness of these principles has been proven by the Beatles themselves!

★ Get in the mood for dreaming! Think about the songs "Strawberry Fields Forever" and "Penny Lane." Reflect on these lyrics: "In Penny Lane the barber shaves another customer, / We see the banker sitting waiting for a trim / And then the fireman rushes in / From the pouring rain—very strange." Such poetry Paul found in this most mundane scene! Scenes from your own life have no less poetry. Let the power of that magical music wash over you, inspiring your own dreams.

★ At the busiest time of your day, stop everything and find a quiet place, preferably in a natural setting, and simply *dream*. If you can't find a forest, a park, or even your own backyard, then go to your car, close the windows and your eyes, and begin dreaming about anything you want to. Like the Beatles, who enjoyed a hearty dream-life in the quiet environs of their Liverpool bedrooms, make this a regular practice. Be wild, untamed, unlimited. Don't edit the dream or doubt that it can come true. Stay with the dream for several minutes.

★ Take out a pen and several pieces of unlined paper. Begin writing down and drawing out your dream. Don't acknowledge negative thoughts. When you're in dreaming mode, the critical you should take a hike. Be free with your pen. Give yourself a full five minutes of moving your pen on the paper without stopping. Even better, buy a box of crayons and fill up a plain notepad with your most colorful imaginings. Be childlike, filled with the promise that your dreams lie in wait as future realities.

★ Hit the library or your local bookstore and grab every book you can on the subjects you're interested in. The Beatles would travel across their entire city to find one record of songs they wanted to learn to play. What about you? Take time to seriously study the subject you love most. Even fifteen minutes a day adds up fast. Ask yourself, how did the people who are masters at your avocation achieve success, and how can you emulate them? Choose one habit or trait they exhibit, and work on consciously incorporating that into your daily life. Check yourself frequently and ask, "What would Hero X (insert your role model's name here) do in this situation?"

★ Look around at your immediate settings, consciously noting everything there, down to the smallest detail—the dishes you eat from, the headlines in the paper, the chatter of children, the scene outside your window. *See* them, don't just look at them. What do they mean? Nothing? You're not in fab mode yet! Everything has meaning, everything is in relation to everything else. What's all around you—in your ears and in your eyes? Watch closely the people around you as they talk, eat, shop, relax. Ask yourself, what can I learn from my environment, and how can I deploy it in creating or realizing my dreams?

2 GOALS

We used to have lots of ambitions.
Like number one records,
"Sunday Night at the London Palladium",
to go to America, to play on "The Ed Sullivan Show."
We're living an awful lot of them.

—Paul McCartney

Like the fledgling "Fab Four" on their way to living their dreams, you too have been doing your creative visualizations, getting your ideas onto paper, and honing up on the skills needed to get your fantasies up and running.

Next on the Beatle success agenda is a biggie: *goal-setting*. While this simple technique is commonly known as the central motivational factor in "getting what you want," quite often it lies neglected, forgotten under the crush of our daily responsibilities.

Not so for the Beatles. Just this one principle kept the group excitedly motivated throughout their entire career. They were relentless on staying focused on a goal and reaching it once they set it. Rarely, if ever, did they not achieve a goal purposely set.

Money as the Initial Goal

"Just give me money—that's what I want..."
("Money," 1963)

All four Beatles were clear on their most important goals, and their very first goal was an obvious one—*making money*. Many of their comments to the press during their early world tours reflect this:

Question: "How do you add up success?"
Beatles (in unison): "Money!"

Question: "What will you do when Beatlemania subsides?"
John: "Count the money!"

Question: "Are you communists?"
Paul: "Us, communists? Why, we can't be communists. We're the world's number one capitalists. Imagine us, communists!"
Ringo: "Anytime you spell 'beetle' with an 'a' in it, we get the money!"

The drive for money may have originated from looking for a way out of their bleak Liverpool. Sure, they had their vivid dreams for becoming the world's next Elvis, but their immediate desire was simply to acquire the money that could buy them the freedom to live where they wanted, as they wanted—as far from their dreaded "Liddypool" as possible.

Young John was often heard exclaiming he'd "do anything" to get out of Liverpool. He later told Beatle biographer Hunter Davies in 1967, "I always felt I'd make it. There were moments of doubt, but I knew something would eventually happen. I had to be a millionaire." He added, "In England, I think people should get their false teeth and their health looked after, but apart from that, I worked for my money and I wanted to be rich."

"The Beatles as anti-materialistic is a huge myth," said Paul, discussing writing hits-on-demand such as "Eight Days a Week." He further noted, "John and I literally used to sit down and say, 'Let's write a swimming pool.'" Paul told reporters in 1965, "We'd be idiots to say it isn't a constant inspiration to be making a lot of money. It always is, to anyone. I mean, why do big business tycoons stay big business tycoons? It's not because they're inspired at the greatness of big business; they're in it because they're making a lot of money at it."

And George added his two cents—pardon the pun—around the same time: "I am interested in money. When I hadn't had much of it, I was just as interested in what a small amount could be made to do."

For many, the subject of money has negative connotations, and terms like "filthy lucre" and "dirty money" come to mind. Others consider the pursuit of money shallow, even selfish. But we all need money to function. Go ask your supermarket manager if you could trade a poem you wrote or some flowers you grew for a bag of groceries. If earning money is what it's going to take to motivate you toward an exciting and compelling life, then so be it. It's nothing to be embarrassed about. For the Beatles, money gave them the freedom to live lavish and experimental lifestyles and also provided them with the clout to back up their artistic endeavors.

And of course, the Beatles' goals matured as their most outrageous money goals were met. "I hate for the Beatles to be remembered as four jovial moptops," Paul said in June 1966, not long before one of their last live concerts, in San Francisco. "I'd like us to be remembered as four people who made music that stands up to be remembered." And Ringo relayed a similar goal: "I'd like to be in school history books and read about by kids."

What's your take on money? For the Beatles, money was—well—OK. They'd seen enough scrimping among their fellow citizens of Liverpool to know that fear or distrust of money was not the wisdom path they wished to follow. Money has its place. Don't let it be your ultimate goal, but don't let guilt and resentment toward money—or those who have it—give you an excuse for stalling dreams you hold precious.

Set Your Goals One Step at a Time

"To the toppermost of the poppermost!"

(Where John would say the group was headed when they were discouraged, 1962)

Before the Fabs could get into the history books, however, they'd have to begin setting some goals. And Beatle goal-setting was done thoughtfully, purposely, systematically. Paul often called the Beatles way to success a staircase climb. Self-help experts advise that goals should not be ridiculously lofty at first. Setting a stratospheric initial goal can lead to discouragement, frustration, and ofttimes, resignation. Sure, the Beatles wanted to be biggest act in show business, but the group approached that overall goal one baby step at a time.

Paul noted in a May 1964 interview with David Frost, "We think of things in stages. When we first started off playing in the 'Cavern' [the local hot club in Liverpool], we thought, 'Next, let's get a record contract.' When we got a record contract, we said, 'Let's get a number-one hit.'"

Frost then asked Paul, "After you got a number-one hit, you hoped for another number-one. Then what?"

Paul replied, "Something like the 'Royal Variety Performance' [an appearance before the queen of England]. Something big. Then—what came after that?—America, I think. And then a film [A *Hard Day's Night* had just been completed]."

Frost persisted, "What about after that?" and Paul jokingly settled the question, "Oh, don't ask me, I'm only doing it!"

George agreed that each Beatle goal was systematically set and met. "The first time I heard 'Love Me Do' on the radio, I went shivery all over. The most important thing in our lives was to get into the Top 20." "Love Me Do" did eventually reach number seventeen on the British charts—not too shabby for the first record of a group from the "sticks," as Londoners originally referred to them. Interestingly, their dream was for a top-twenty hit, not a number-one or a top-ten hit.

On the Beatle-goal methodology, John was in total synch with Paul and George: "[First] we wanted to make it big in Liverpool, to be the best group in the county. Then, being the best group in England, we went to Scotland to break them in, things like that. The goal was always a few yards ahead, rather than way up there."

Goal-work was an essential part of the Beatles way. And despite the incredible heights of success they achieved, their goals were never outlandish; rather, they were reasonable and never intimidating. Are your goals set too high? If so, you might never take action on them for fear of never achieving them. Fab wisdom means setting goals one step at a time, exponentially attaining small goals on your way to realizing your big-picture dream.

Doing Whatever It Takes
"I've been working like a dog..."
("A Hard Day's Night," 1964)

Imagine this kind of pressure. It's a cold February morning in London (February 11, 1963). You wake up groggy after having performed the night before in a remote town a hundred miles north. You have a number-one song on the charts ("Please Please Me"), and the corporate powers-that-be have decided to produce an album with you at the lowest possible expense before your group slides off the charts and out of people's memories. Worse, one of your lead singers (John Lennon) is as sick as the proverbial dog with a heavy flu from endless winter touring. You know you've got to pull off this album or it's back to the Liverpool clubs or worse. What to do if you're truly fab?

First, you show up at the studio at 10 A.M.; unpack your instruments; dip into the day's supply of tea, milk, and "Zubes" throat lozenges; and let loose with one of the most powerful live performances in rock history. Beginning with "There's a Place" and quickly moving on to "I Saw Her Standing There," you finally finish the tenth and last song a full twelve hours later with a near-apocalyptic version of "Twist and Shout," with your flu-ravaged singer throat-shredded, sweating, and stripped to the waist.

In today's yearlong, multitrack, computer-centric music recording, this emotionally wrenching single day of live recording stands as legendary, nearly forty years later. But this is the sort of astounding preparedness typical of the Beatles throughout their career. They would never merely just "show up" for work. They were always ready, willing, and able to pour out every ounce of energy needed to be exceptional—even explosive—in what they wished to accomplish. In fact, after that late-night "Twist and Shout" performance at Abbey Road's EMI Recording Studios, the small group of studio engineers gave the group a standing ovation, whooping and hollering in honor of the massive effort of all four Beatles.

The mettle the group showed in recording their first album is palpable. They had good reasons to cancel the session or to cut it off at a reasonable hour. Instead, they rolled up their sleeves and gave the performance of their lives.

In this day and age of entitlement, this attitude of doing WIT ("whatever it takes") to meet a goal is rare indeed. It's the Beatles way. Let it be your way, too.

How would you have handled this situation? How are you handling the work involved in meeting your goals? If you give up too soon on them, perhaps your goals aren't exciting enough to really motivate you. Perhaps you need to dream up new ones that really move you and keep you giving *whatever it takes*.

Never Give Up on Your Dreams
"Yes I will, I'll get you in the end ..."
("I'll Get You," 1963)

While we're studying the Beatles way of goal-setting, let's take it a step up now to discover exactly what separated the wheat from the chaff, the men from the boys, the Beatles from the Freddie and the Dreamers. Yes, you say, you've been dreaming, you've set some dreams down on paper, and you've even started setting some realistic goals. And you're willing to do *whatever it takes* to achieve those dreams. Are you absolutely, unequivocally certain about that?

Once the Fabs decided to live out their dream to become "bigger than Elvis, " there would be no turning back. There was not a moment spent entertaining indecision, doubt, or regret, never a thought to quitting, no matter what happened. In making that decision, the road before them, literally, was going to be a long and arduous one. Let's look at just how dedicated the Beatles were in the literal *work* of making their dreams come true:

★ From 1960 to 1966, the Beatles logged a total of 1,400 performances. That's an average of 233 per year.

★ The group adhered to a rigorous schedule of record releases: four singles and two albums—that's thirty-plus songs—per year during the Beatlemania days. From 1964 to 1966, they released twelve albums in America and five in Great Britain.

★ During August and September 1964, on their second U.S. tour, the group traveled 22,441 miles. That's 60½ hours of flying while visiting twenty-four cities in the United States and Canada for a total of thirty-one performances.

★ In less than six months in 1966, the Beatles visited and performed in fifty cities on four continents.

Let's break it down and go year-by-year on this astounding pace of doing whatever it takes:

★ *1963:* The Beatles recorded thirty songs, including the albums *Please Please Me* and *With the Beatles* and the singles "She Loves You" and "I Want to Hold Your Hand." They played a *Sunday Night at the London Palladium* television performance for 20 million people and a "Royal Command Performance" before the queen of England, and they toured Europe.

★ *1964:* The group recorded thirty-five songs for the albums *A Hard Day's Night* and *Beatles for Sale* as well as several singles. They played *The Ed Sullivan Show* for 73 million viewers and toured the United States and the world. They also filmed the movie *A Hard Day's Night.*

★ *1965:* The Beatles recorded thirty-three songs for the albums *Help!* and *Rubber Soul* as well as more singles, on top of more world touring. They filmed the movie *Help!* The album *Rubber Soul* was begun October 12 and finished November 15, a remarkable feat.

★ *1966:* The Fabs recorded nineteen songs, including the breakthrough *Revolver* album and the single "Paperback Writer." Another world tour was undertaken. The double-A-sided single (meaning both songs were of the highest quality) "Strawberry Fields Forever/Penny Lane" was begun in December.

★ *1967:* The group recorded twenty-five songs, including the albums *Sgt. Pepper's Lonely Hearts Club Band* and *Magical Mystery Tour*, and filmed the movie *Magical Mystery Tour.* The group began recording songs for *Magical Mystery Tour* four days after finishing *Sgt. Pepper*, and they recorded the single "All You Need Is Love" a mere five weeks after finishing the *Pepper* album as well as performing the song for 400 million viewers on a global television broadcast.

★ *1968:* The Fab Four recorded thirty-seven songs for the *White Album* and worked on the movie *Yellow Submarine* and the accompanying soundtrack. They recorded the "Hey Jude" single, taped twenty-three demos for the *White Album* in one day (May 30) at George's home recording studio, began their own business (Apple Corps Ltd.), and produced records for several Apple artists.

★ *1969:* The Beatles recorded twenty-nine songs, including the *Let It Be* and *Abbey Road* albums, and filmed the movie *Let It Be*, and all four began independent projects.

"We never stopped!" said Ringo, reflecting on the early days of the group's success. "If we were in Elgin on a Thursday, but needed to be in Portsmouth on Friday [northern Scotland to southern England], we would just drive, we didn't know how to stop, this band. Some nights it would be so foggy, we'd be doing one mile an hour, and we'd still just keep *going*."

Paul gave another example of the intense dedication the group had mastered toward their goals: "I remember the tour van's windscreen got knocked out, and Mal Evans [driver and roadie] turned his hat around, punched the windscreen out, and just drove on. This was winter in Britain, and it was freezing. We were very, very cold, and we'd lay on each other for warmth."

An interview from the Beatles' first American tour in 1964 reveals their no-nonsense ultra-dedication mind-set:

Question: "Are you disappointed in your American tour because you're forced to spend so much time in seclusion because of your fans?"
George: "We expect on any tour we do to be secluded and not have much of a chance to see the cities."
John (sharply): "Because we're here to work."

Yes indeed, they were here to work. With Beatlemania already having raged for eighteen months in the United Kingdom, the Beatles landed in London on February 22, 1964, after their ten-day conquest of America (two *Ed Sullivan* shows and three live concerts). The very next day, they tele-recorded six live songs and three comedy sketches for the television show *Big Night Out*. After one day off, and one week before shooting commenced on *A Hard Day's Night*, the group met at Abbey Road Studios to record songs for the film.

One little-known fact of Beatle dedication occurred during the filming of the recording of *Let It Be* in 1969 on the rooftop of the Apple building.

After this emotional and climactic performance, the group immediately went downstairs and filmed the final versions of "Let It Be," "Two of Us," and "The Long and Winding Road." The rooftop concert should've been exhausting enough. They hadn't played live in years, they were in the midst of a stressful and sometimes acrimonious breakup, it was a freezing day, and the police had threatened arrest unless the group shut down the concert. However, for the Beatles, it was all in a day's work.

The willingness to do whatever it took to achieve their dream is central to the Beatles legacy, as you can see in the amount of work they accomplished in their career. A simple formula can be applied here: the bigger the dream, the bigger the workload.

On first look at your own dream, the amount of work might overwhelm you. But just remember what Paul said, and view your journey toward success as a "staircase climb." When you are moving one small and purposeful step at a time up a stairwell, even a gigantic dream is manageable. You couldn't leap to the top of the 555-foot-tall Washington Monument in one jump. But you can get there by taking it one step— all 897 of them—at a time. One famous Buddhist exercise is to actually walk as slowly as humanly possible in order to focus on the tiniest movement made forward. Focusing on the small step in front of you, as the Beatles did, makes goal-reaching enjoyable and manageable. There's no need to get overwhelmed by the size of the dream you're looking to accomplish.

Always Be Prepared
"All together now..."
("All You Need Is Love," 1968)

Let's take a closer look at how the Beatles adopted a perennial state of readiness, always prepared for the biggest moments in their career.

A little-known related fact on their preparedness concerns the short speech by John at the all-important "Royal Command Performance" in November 1963 before the queen of England and other British royalty. While many believe John's speech was improvised, he had rehearsed it. In fact, John's pithy "For those in the cheap seats, just clap your hands. The rest of you, if you'll just rattle your jewelry" was causing manager Brian Epstein much consternation hours before the show, as John jokingly threatened to spice up his joke with a pointedly-placed expletive. To Epstein's delight, John wisely didn't use the term "fookin' jewelry" on that all-important night.

And how about trooper George? Sick with a flu on the first visit to the United States, he handled the group's initial press conference at JFK Airport with seeming ease and only a day later pulled himself together with a ready smile to perform for 73 million viewers on *The Ed Sullivan Show*. That kind of recovery under intense pressure can only happen when you're totally prepared, when you've got your act down cold.

On a more workaday note, preparedness was an integral factor in keeping the Beatles comfortable while living inside the eye of the Beatlemania hurricane. Here's the actual list that concert promoters received months before a Beatles appearance:

★ For security, at least one hundred uniformed police officers.
★ A hi-fidelity sound system with an adequate number of speakers.
★ Four floor-stand hi-fi microphones, and 40 feet of cord for each microphone.
★ A first class sound engineer.
★ The dimensions of the stage are to be not less than 25 feet square and at least five feet high.
★ Clean and adequate dressing room facilities.
★ Four cots, mirrors, ice cooler, and portable TV set, and clean towels.
★ Two passenger Cadillac limousines, air conditioned, if possible.

Nat Weiss, the Beatles' attorney during the Beatlemania years, sums up why this list was worked out well in advance of the tours: "It was done out of necessity, not ego. We were pretty sure that once we got the group inside [the dressing area], there wouldn't be any way for them to come and go as they pleased, they would have to stay put, maybe for long hours." Indeed, preparation was key for the group.

How organized are you in your own goal-setting? Sure, dreaming, setting goals, and working hard are necessary ingredients, but as the Beatles knew, being prepared—both emotionally and physically—is also integral. Are you prepared for any unexpected challenge that might pop up to try and thwart your attempt to reach your goal?

Keeping Pace with Your Dream

"Baby, now you're movin' way too fast..."
("Slow Down," 1963)

There's a term in the business world used to assess a company's performance in creating and then delivering a finished product to the public. This "time-to-market" is crucial, as a company's competitors are often working on accomplishing the same goal. However, for the Beatles, time-to-market was never a problem. This group moved too fast. The time from when the Fabs recorded "Love Me Do" to the release of "Strawberry Fields Forever" was a little over four years, yet there was a quantum-like growth in their musical development. Impatience was inherent in the Beatle consciousness. They were ever wishing to change, to grow, to move, to get on with the new and leave the old behind.

Paul recalled this amazing pace: "The whole *Please Please Me* album [recorded in twelve hours] only took a day... so it was amazingly cheap, no-messing, just a massive effort from us. But we were game. We'd been to Hamburg, for God's sake, we'd stayed up all night, it was no big deal. We started at ten in the morning and finished at ten at night—it sounded like a working day to us! And at the end of the day you had your album. There's many a person now who would love to be able to say that, me included."

Actually, the group nearly did repeat the time-to-market accomplishment of *Please Please Me* with their *Sgt. Pepper* album, which took just four months from start to finish. Compare this with today's industry standard of taking a full year to record a new album by a hit act and spending millions of dollars on production and promotion.

Additionally, the group made the film *A Hard Day's Night* in 1964 for less than $350,000 in just over seven weeks. Don't even bother boggling your mind with how this relates to today's era of $100 million movie-production costs and yearlong shoots. "It was a blur. Nobody had time to stop and think over what they were doing," said Richard Lester, the film's director. "But the incredible speed with which it was made worked to its benefit."

But to the Beatles, the grueling pace was no big deal. Paul explained, "Seven or eight weeks was a long time in our life, equivalent to a year. We could have done a couple of tours, written a few new songs and cut an album, maybe even have done a few other things. But to the people working on the set, it was a comparatively short time. We didn't know any better, we just thought, 'Wow! This is taking a long time!'"

The reason for the rush job? Simple: United Artists and the Beatles' record company were concerned over the possibility that their investment would be lost if the group peaked in popularity before the movie's release. The movie's title only officially became *A Hard Day's Night* on July 13, 1964. And at 8:30 A.M. the very next day, John and Paul were playing the finished song in their dressing room for the movie's producer, Walter Shenson, and recording it two days later. Richard Lester stated they pulled a similar feat for their next movie, writing and recording the song "Help!" in only thirty hours after the title was decided upon.

Paul summed up the Beatle determination to do whatever it took and to get their music to their audience as fast as possible. "I think the Beatles were *on*," he said. "I can't really use any other word, they were just *on*." He added, "There was no question of any hang-ups interfering with it, because we had an understanding, we were all aiming for the same thing."

John gave an honest account of the hard work it took to get where they wanted to be: "Don't you think the Beatles gave every soddin' thing they had to be the Beatles? That took a whole section of our youth. That period when everybody was just goofing off, we were working twenty-four hours a day." Point of fact: On the night of August 23, 1962, the day John married Cynthia Powell, his art-school sweetheart, he was playing in the tiny town of Chester, England. For the Beatles, honeymoons could wait. Goals couldn't!

I'm not suggesting sacrificing your own wedding night to your goals, but the Beatles were out to keep up with the responsibilities their dream demanded once they set it in motion.

Are you willing to keep the proverbial carrot in front of you as you chase your wildest dreams? Fab wisdom says, "Yeah!"

The Power of a Personal Incubator
"Mach Schau! Mach Schau!"
(What the crowd shouted as the Beatles performed onstage for six to eight hours in Germany—
"Make show! Make show!")

Whew! Hold on there. Let's reflect for just a minute. Just how do you drive yourself to do what the Beatles did? How do you find the stamina within—the dedication, the energy, the strength—to physically just *do* it?

We can find some clues in the Beatles' well-documented residence in Hamburg, Germany, in 1960–61, when they worked as a club band. This

Hamburg interlude burnished the Beatles from a scruffy, amateurish beat group into a world-class entertainment machine. It was there that the four leather-clad determinists became not only hardened entertainers but also survivalists. Hamburg was just the right incubator to grow the strength, stamina, and tenacity that the Beatles would need to carry them through the Beatlemania hurricane and beyond.

In chapter 5, "Control," we'll look at the priceless artistry that came out of the group's interaction with Hamburg artist/photographers Astrid Kirchherr, Klaus Voorman, and Jurgen Vollmer and how it helped them present a unique image to the world. But for now, let's take a look at the impact of Hamburg as a trial by fire.

Incredibly, in five trips to the country over a two-year period, the Beatles spent an estimated eight hundred total hours onstage in Hamburg. Paul said in 1963 of the experience, "Back home in Liverpool we'd only done hour-long shows, so we just did our best numbers over and over again. But in Hamburg, we had to play for eight hours a night, so we really had to find a new way of playing."

This new way of playing included turning their simple rock 'n' roll act into a crowd-rousing event night after grueling night. Fueled by beer, uppers, and sheer manic fervor, they stomped, hollered, and staged mock fights, all in response to the drunken seaport crowd shouting, "Mach Schau! Mach Schau!"

The only comfort for the four overworked teens was in sleep. Unfortunately, their living quarters were located directly behind the movie-theater screen of the club they were working in, complete with bunk beds, Union Jack flags for bed sheets, rats, and roaches.

However, when the Fabs returned to play for their hometown audience in 1962, the change in their act was marked. Fans began screaming for the first time, and lines formed around the block outside the clubs the day before a show. The Beatles have all emphasized that the Hamburg experience gave them the tenacity and strength to take whatever the world threw at them.

In working toward achieving your own dreams, think about creating your own personal incubator. This might be obvious for certain job tasks such as computer programmers who run codes through a variety of tests before a software release or for automotive engineers who test cars with crash-test dummies before allowing companies to produce and sell the cars.

Suppose you'd like to become a stand-up comedian? Sure, you break up all your buddies at the office, but heading out to the local comedy clubs and standing on an actual stage in front of strangers is an entirely different experience. It's the real deal. But only with that kind of incubator—where you can hone your act, learn from others, and network into the industry—will you be following the Beatles way.

Perhaps you've been thinking about going back to college for your master's degree in teaching. Sure, with the dedication and time commitment needed to achieve the M.A., you'll surely secure the lambskin required. But go further. Have you thought about the big day when you walk in front of thirty to forty people and have to teach them in a way that will truly reach and inspire them? Why not do some volunteer work to start off with, and give your teaching talent some time to shine? Think about how an incubator could help you in practicing up on your dreams, just as it proved so useful for the Beatles in Hamburg.

Taking Courage
"You Can't Do That"
(*A Hard Day's Night*, 1964)

The Hamburg experience gave the Beatles something else: a warrior mentality. After they survived the grueling hours in a foreign city with little or no money and with only their wit and talent to carry them through, you can bet that no one ever again got the chance to order them about or to take advantage of them. No *way.*

"At the beginning, we were four guys that gave all our energy to this entity called the Beatles, and we *fought*," said Ringo years later. "John and Paul fought for our songs, and we put all of our energy into it. And there was nothing else to get in the way." Determination became a hallmark of the Beatles way, as at nearly every step, someone in power wanted a piece of their dream done differently.

The first battle came directly after their initial recording sessions with producer George Martin. Even though "Love Me Do" had become a top-twenty hit, Martin, an experienced producer, wanted them to cover a song written by seasoned pop songwriter Mitch Murray, who was later to be known for "Hitchin' a Ride" and "Billy Don't Be a Hero."

The song in question was "How Do You Do It," a catchy ditty with perhaps too-clever lyrics such as "You give me a feeling in my heart, like an arrow passing through it." This glib sentiment reflected none of the Beatles outright emotional honesty in their own work. Paul remembered, "We didn't like it, and we came back to George Martin and said, 'Well it may be a number one, but we just don't want this kind of song, we don't want to go out with that kind of reputation.'"

That was pretty courageous talk from the fledgling Fabs, but they did have what it took to back their words up. Accordingly, a month later, after giving EMI its due by recording "How Do You Do It" in Beatle-style, they sat George Martin down on his high stool and performed "Please Please Me." George Martin knew he had his number-one Beatle record then and there. "How Do You Do It" went unreleased.

"Occasionally, we'd overrule George Martin," noted Paul. "Like on 'She Loves You,' which we ended with a sixth chord, a very jazzy sort of thing. And he said, 'Oh, you can't do that! A sixth chord? It's too jazzy.' We said, 'No, it's a great hook, we've *got* to do it!'" That kind of confidence when you're being challenged by others comes only after you've let yourself be tested by fire.

Another ongoing battle presented itself with something as obvious as the way the Beatles spoke. In England, a near–caste system gave proper English urbanites a reason to mock the group's Northern accents. But the Beatles were not to be molded. They prevailed, ultimately charming the world with their Liverpudlian speech. "We were the first working-class singers that stayed working class," said John. "We didn't try and change our accents, which were looked down upon in England, and probably still are." Even years into the group's fame, they had to resist others' ideas on what their success would look like. *A Hard Day's Night* producer Walter Shenson remembered a call from American representatives at United Artists (the film's distributor) who insisted that the group's voices be dubbed over with "professional" ones. The Beatles once again had to stand their ground, and firmly.

Let's look at the Beatles' ideas for their album covers. Now considered perhaps the most creative presentation for a recording in history, the *With the Beatles* cover depicts the Fabs' faces in half-shadow. It was railed against by the record company. Representatives at EMI called it "shockingly humorless." One marketing executive said, "Where is the fun? Why are they looking so grim? We want to project happy Beatles for happy fans!" It took a full-scale battle for the Beatles to prevail. It was courage forged by their own determination and inner knowing that helped the Beatles keep their goals in control.

And the cover for *Sgt. Pepper*, which depicts dozens of celebrities and heroes handpicked by the Beatles themselves, caused so much consternation for manager Brian Epstein and the high levels of corporate EMI that Brian, in his last official act as the Beatles' manager, wrote them a personal note calling for the album to be distributed in "plain brown wrappers."

Paul said that EMI chairman Sir Joseph Lockwood visited him at home, exclaiming, "There are going to be problems with all these people, all these faces, because everyone has the right to their own likeness and you can't just put them on a cover. They're going to sue us! We're going to be up to our eyeballs in lawsuits!"

Paul fought back: "No you won't! What you should do is ring them all and ask them! Have you rung them all?" "No," Lockwood replied. Paul had to lay out the steps for EMI to take: "Well, ring Marlon Brando, or his agent, and say, 'The Beatles would love him to be on this montage on the front. It's an homage to these people.' Explain it!" Again, after a hard-fought skirmish, the Beatles won out. The cover for *Sgt. Pepper's Lonely Hearts Club Band* stands as perhaps the most imaginative and influential presentation ever created.

The Beatles' belief in their own vision had a profound effect on the world recording industry. Initially, the Fabs had submitted to the standard music-business practice of re-recording vocal parts in other languages on big hits. In fact, they sang "I Want to Hold Your Hand" and "She Loves You" in German. However, they quickly tired of this unnatural process and decided to drop it. Despite pressure, they stood by that decision. That single act precipitated the end, industrywide, of the practice. More important, the effect was the virtual worldwide promotion of the English language, one of the Beatles' most substantial but underdocumented achievements.

How willing are you to stand up for your dream? How often do you find yourself saying, "You've got to pick your battles," and giving up on some crucial point of a goal? Next time, try the Beatles way: Speak from your heart the truth of what you believe. You'll be surprised at the results. Quite often, the person who's got "other ideas" about something you feel strongly about will back down in the face of your courage and spirit and will often just say, "OK, fine, sure, we can do it your way!"

Enjoying the Fruits of Your Labors
"A Taste of Honey"
(*Please Please Me*, 1963)

Following the Beatles way, it's obvious that lots of hard work, tenacity, and hard-fought battles are crucial components in making it to the "toppermost of the poppermost." Let's look at the flip side of this methodology. If we can get spiritual for a moment, Jesus was fond of saying to his disciples, "Man cannot live by bread alone." For the Beatles, that gospel was true indeed.

Accordingly, the group enjoyed the fruits of their labors to a very lofty degree. All bought huge houses in exclusive areas of England, expensive clothes, art, and luxury cars. In fact, John's celebrated Rolls-Royce cost $25,000—a fortune in the '60s—and he had it painted in an outrageous psychedelic collage, with flowers on the door panels and the signs of the zodiac on the roof. George purchased luxury cars, including a Ferrari, a Porsche, a Lamborghini, a Rolls-Royce, a BMW, and a customized Mercedes. Paul spent thousands to purchase his father a well-known winning racehorse, "Drake's Drum." In fact, when he presented a picture of the horse to him, Paul's dad initially thought the gift was the framed picture itself, and Paul had to say with amazement, "No! I bought you the bloody horse, Dad!"

Additionally, directly after their strenuous recording sessions, which usually ran into the wee hours, all four would party in London's after-hours nightclubs. But for John and Paul, a more artistic muse was to be satisfied. Both were attracted to the underground art scene in London in the mid-'60s. The two made frequent visits to their favorite art gallery, Indica, where John met Yoko Ono in 1966. Paul loved the gallery so much he would pitch in with physical labor occasionally, doing carpentry, painting, and spackling.

The Beatles also enjoyed how their fame allowed them to participate in outside projects not directly related to group business. Paul and George wrote and produced soundtrack albums—Paul for *The Family Way*, a successful Hayley Mills vehicle, and George for the experimental *Wonderwall* film soundtrack.

John and Ringo took their turn at acting, and John also found time to write and publish two books of his own artwork and poetry. "I had a professional songwriter's attitude toward writing pop songs," said John of his extracurricular work, "but to express myself [fully], I would write *A Spaniard in the Works* or *In His Own Write*, [two books which included] stories expressive of my personal emotions."

George's interest in Hinduism during the height of Beatlemania often led him to trekking to India to study with gurus and master musicians. His devotion to Hinduism endures to this day. In fact, in 1997, George produced one of the best-selling Ravi Shankar albums of all time, *Chants*.

In the spirit of the Beatles way, after you realize a goal, you should do something wonderful for yourself! Did you finally see the results of your goal-setting, and it's manifested into your life in a beautiful way? Did you get that new car you've been dreaming of? Did you get the promotion at work you really wanted? Well, great! Throw a party! Take a few days off and go on a short vacation. Buy yourself something silly! As the Beatles so often did during their remarkable career of achievements—celebrate!

Significant Others
"She's a Woman"
(*Help*, 1965)

Despite the temptations of throngs of young women at their beck and call, for most of their public lives, the Beatles were "one-woman men." In fact,

John married his art-college sweetheart, Cynthia Powell, at age twenty-two and quickly had an infant to care for right at the beginnings of the group's early success. After the two parted ways, it wasn't even a heartbeat's time until John took up with his newest creative catalyst, Yoko Ono, who single-handedly rekindled John's creative passions in the late '60s and sent his financial fortune to new heights in the mid-'70s.

Then we have George, who fell in love immediately with *A Hard Day's Night* extra and professional model Patti Boyd, eventually marrying her within a year. And ditto Ringo, who married Liverpool girlfriend Maureen Cox in 1965 after a lengthy courtship. Paul was smitten for years with British actress Jane Asher, and she was influential in introducing him to the avant-garde scene in London. And due to her upper-class upbringing, Jane was also able to offer the somewhat naïve Paul a real hands-on education in leading a sophisticated and elegant lifestyle.

And it was on the heels of his breakup with Jane that Paul met the woman with whom he was to be married for thirty years, Linda Eastman. Paul has said publicly many times that Linda revitalized him after the breakup of the Beatles and inspired him to continue his musical career, which saw another twenty years of success with his group Wings and with his solo legacy through the '70s and '80s.

Do you have a significant other in your life? Is your partner in synch with your dreams? Your husband? Your wife? If you're not getting the support you need to make your goals a reality, it might be a good time to get on the same page with your partner regarding this all-important matter. The integral women in the Beatles' lives provided more than companion-ship—and were much more than cooks, housewives, or lovers. These women were independent in their own right and were often the inspira-tion of—or hands-on collaborator in—many of the Beatles' important songs. Living life the Beatles' way means being open to a love and relationship that will empower you to reach for your dreams.

YOU'RE THE FIFTH BEATLE! — *Goals*

Let's do a few exercises that will help you in taking the Beatles way of setting and meeting goals:

★ Mach Schau! Mach Schau! Right now—this minute—jump up and put on the loudest rock 'n' roll number you have from a Beatles album. Perhaps it's "Twist and Shout" or "Roll Over Beethoven" or "Long Tall Sally." Sing the song at the top of your lungs! Go crazy with it. Dance around your house or apartment as the young Beatles so often did on their Hamburg stages. This will help you free up any inhibitions you perceive you might have before you begin your goal-setting session.

★ Ask yourself, what's your most compelling goal? What's going to get you excited enough to *move* on an action plan? For the young Beatles, their first goal was a simple one—money. However, for you, it might be a new car, a new relationship, or finding meaningful work. Whatever your goals are, list them and break them down, step by step.

★ Like the Beatles, are your goals set up in a staircase climb? Review your list. Are your steps achievable? Will you be willing to keep moving forward even after achieving your preliminary goals? Don't get too comfortable now!

★ Are you willing to do *whatever it takes* to achieve your goals? How prepared are you in undertaking the manifesting of your dreams? Are you physically fit enough to take on the work your dream will require in order to see it manifest? Are you prepared emotionally to deal with success? Failure? Take your goals and the work needed to achieve them very seriously. A casual attitude won't cut it.

★ How willing are you to keep your dream pure? Are you willing to trust your instincts in order to achieve what you *feel* and *know* is perfect for you and your dream—as the Beatles did so often — despite massive pressure to the contrary? Don't let others co-opt your dream. Your hard work will make you strong and able to resist others' incursion on your ideal.

3 ATTITUDE

I think we must have been pretty tough,
because I've heard of people cracking up
and having nervous breakdowns with
not even a fraction of what we went through.

—George Harrison

Being fab means having attitude. Big-time attitude. Just listen to John Lennon in 1971. His attitude gets right in your face the minute he's asked how he accomplished so much in his young life. "Because I fuckin' *did* it!" he exclaimed. "Have you ever heard of artists like Dylan Thomas [the Welsh poet] or Brendan Behan [Irish writer and playwright], and all the rest, who never wrote [to their potential] but went up drinking? I came out of the sticks. I hadn't heard about anything. Van Gogh was the most far-out thing I'd ever heard of. Even London was something we used to dream of, and London's nothing. I came out of the fuckin' sticks to take over the world!"

Wow! That's attitude. And as you might expect, being fab takes attitude one step further. It goes deeper, to an inner knowingness, a sheer and unquestioning belief in oneself. Doubt rarely, if ever, entered into the Beatle success equation.

You can do one of two things under intense pressure. You can either become nervous, stress out, and give up, or like the Beatles, you can find your inner Olympian strength and make it through the "test," landing squarely on the winner's podium. Let's take a look at the group's attitude and learn from them how to reach deep within ourselves to find that inner strength.

Overcoming Fear of the Unknown
"Tomorrow Never Knows"
(*Revolver*, 1966)

There are two central themes that comprise the Beatle attitude for excelling under intense pressure. John discussed one of these when asked why people have difficulty in actively pursuing their dreams. "It's *fear of the unknown*," he said, "but the unknown is *what it is*. To be frightened of it is what sends everybody scurrying around chasing illusions. Wars, peace, love, hate, all of that, that's all illusion. *Unknown is what it is*. Accept that it's all unknown and it's plain sailing. Know that everything is unknown, and you're ahead of the game."

Some might say that having an attitude is merely a philosophical ideal and not germane to a success methodology, but think of the practical benefits of John's advice. If you can accept that around every corner lies the unknown, this could flip-flop your fear of change. It could mean that you have nothing to lose when pursuing your dream—because, if you really ponder this, just what *is* around the corner that's making you tentative and afraid to take action? Is it something tangible? Or is it merely your *perception* of something dark and terrible that lies in wait there?

Take a hard look at your willingness to pursue your goals. Do you have a lifelong fear of failure? Fear of success? Fear of getting hurt, physically or emotionally? Are these fears justified? Maybe they were—once upon a time. But being fab says that around the next corner, the unknown could just as easily be a wondrous experience waiting to happen, bringing you *joy* or *freedom*. Why should the unknown be something that demands to be feared? It's obvious the Beatles didn't think that way. Why should you?

Emotional Detachment
"I'm Looking Through You"
(*Rubber Soul*, 1966)

The other theme to the Beatle attitude is deceptively simple: *emotional detachment*. Here's George reflecting on this subject during the early days of Beatlemania: "We do enjoy reading the publicity about us, but from time to time you don't actually realize it's about yourself. You see your pictures and read about 'George Harrison,' but you don't actually think, 'Oh, that's me. There I am in the paper!' It's funny, it's just as though it's a different person."

John's detachment and attitude came through loud and clear after the Beatles' Washington D.C. concert in 1964, four days after landing on American soil. A network television reporter, pointing to a video camera, asked, "Well, John, here is the American public. There are the forty million American viewers watching you right now!"

John replied, totally nonplussed, "It only looks like one man to me—the cameraman!"

Paul added his insight to this detachment issue, commenting on his own phenomenal fame: "Occasionally, I stop and think, 'I am *Paul McCartney*, fuckin' hell! This is a total freakout!' You know—*Paul McCartney*! Just the words—it sounds like a total kind of legend. But of course, you don't want to go thinking that much, because it takes over. I think it helps keep you sane actually, if your famous side is removed from you yourself. You can withdraw from it. You can go home after a Beatles session and switch off. I don't think we had any huge problems like some of the stars who couldn't switch identities off."

How emotional do you become under pressure? Try the Beatles way of laughing at yourself and not taking the pressure too seriously. When they worked, they gave it their complete attention and talents. When they were done working at the end of the day, they let it go. Your life's too short not to have that attitude.

No Pressure under Pressure
"You've Got to Hide Your Love Away"
(*Help!*, 1965)

If you can muster this Beatle attitude—acceptance of the unknown with an emotional detachment from the pressures of life—then you can begin to accomplish your own goals, and under the most intense of pressure, just as the Beatles did. In fact, for the Fabs, there was *no pressure under pressure.*

The press was no small task to win over, either. Unlike today's specialized press, the Beatles had to deal with the mainstream media, heavily stacked with jaded, aging reporters comfortable with their local beats of politics, crime, and the latest Hollywood scandal. Most of the press treated the Beatles as a joke or, at best, a novelty act. The pressure to make a good impression was enormous when the Beatles first arrived in the United States in 1964. But for them, it was again no pressure under pressure. They reacted swiftly, professionally, and seemingly without effort. At the group's first U.S. press conference, the four looked perfectly relaxed, if a bit disheveled. They were eager to please and able to fire off hilarious one-line answers to insipid questions.

Let's check out a handful of this ability to "send it up" with wisecracks, these from the famed first U.S. press conference in 1964:

Question: "Will you sing a song for us?"
John: "No, we need money first!"

Question: "One of your songs is 'Roll Over Beethoven.' What do you think of Beethoven as a composer?"

Ringo: "He's great. Especially his poems."

Question: "Why do millions of Beatles fans buy millions of Beatles records?"
John: "If we knew, we'd form another group and become managers!"

Beatle attitude also included charming the world's royalty and political elite. Every country or city the Fabs visited offered up a set of bigwigs who desired nothing less than to associate themselves with the Beatles and who were rarely disappointed.

How would you conduct yourself when meeting important people, a skeptical press, or a throng of fans scrambling for your autograph? Would you be fab—ever ready with a pithy comment and a beaming smile?

OK, so maybe you won't be asked for an autograph, but you can still take this attitude toward your everyday work. You'd like to be promoted at your job? Try the Beatles way: consistently call up a sunny smile and be positive and excellent in your words, manner, and work when you're at the office.

The Beatles actually seemed to seek out pressure by trying the untried. They were the first to hold a world satellite-enabled live television show ("Our World" on June 25, 1967), performing John's "All You Need Is Love" before an estimated 400 million viewers in twenty-four countries on five continents. Live, on the spot. No room for mistakes. But watch the film of that appearance, and there's Paul, sitting cross-legged, nonplussed; George, confident and stately; Ringo, smiling all the while; and John, snapping calmly on a piece of gum as he sings the lead vocal, his body poised in a determined but easy manner.

Check your emotional status. What's your reaction when something goes wrong or appears to be daunting? Do you get upset and want to avoid the emotion building up inside? On the flip side, what about when something goes just the way you want it to? Do you take it in stride, on the way toward realizing your dream, or do you get bigheaded and just a little too cocky? For the Beatles, an even, consistent emotional detachment, inner knowingness concerning their abilities, and confidence in achieving their dreams were an integral component of their power.

Facing Confrontation

"And nothing to get hung about…"
("Strawberry Fields Forever," 1967)

Another pressure the Beatles faced with aplomb was threat to their physical safety. It all started with something as unassuming as jellybeans. Apparently fans had read in teen magazines that the group favored jelly babies as their fave candy. In the United Kingdom, these colorful sweets are soft marshmallow confections. Not so in the United States, where jellybeans are rock-hard, bullet-sized pellets. In their U.S. visits, fans began throwing jellybeans at the group to attract their attention. Films of the group's early U.S. performances reveal these rock candies bouncing sharply off the group's heads and faces as they continued to bravely smile and perform as if nothing of the sort was actually happening.

Next time you're facing a hot situation, get yourself a little visual aid: buy a pack of jellybeans!

When you see old films of the Beatles' confident and carefree performances, it's easy to forget that they feared for their own safety. John F. Kennedy had just been assassinated, beginning a string of violent deaths of famous and controversial men. George Martin noted that as early as 1964, there were increasing concerns to this end. "Before their concert at the Red Rocks Stadium in Denver, Brian and I climbed up one of the lighting towers that straddled the stage. From our bird's-eye vantage point, a cold feeling spread through my stomach. I looked across at Brian. From the look on his face, I could see the same thought had occurred to him—

that a sniper could pick off any one of them at will. President Kennedy's assassination the previous year had made us realize that such horrors were all too possible."

The Beatles played Dallas months after JFK's assassination there. As fans packed the street, during the ride in from Dallas's Love Field to the hotel, the Beatles' motorcade followed the same route as the Kennedy motorcade—past the Texas School Book Depository and through the infamous underpass, the exact place where Kennedy had been shot and killed less than a year before. According to their accompanying photographer, all the Beatles remarked about this when the car hit that patch of eerily familiar territory, but they were still able to offer onlookers a smile and a wave. The group played a sold-out concert that same night.

There were constant bomb threats during the Beatles' second U.S. tour. George recounted several stories in his biography, *I Me Mine*: "There were occasions when we were supposed to jump in the car to go and make our escapes, but the cars got jumped on, and the roofs were squashed down to the seats. All kinds of horrors started happening during Beatlemania, like when we were in Canada. The French were having an argument with the British, and they decided that when we were coming to Montreal, somebody was going to shoot Ringo! Our nervous system was taking a real beating."

George also told of other violence against them: "There was a pilot I met in the '70s, while I was on a plane from New York to Los Angeles. And he said, 'George, you don't remember me, but I'm the pilot from the American Flyers Electra plane [which the Beatles used on their early U.S. tours].' He said, 'You'd never believe that plane! It was just full of bullet holes—the tails, and the wings, everything—just full of bullet holes!' And I said, 'How come?' He said that when the Beatles were arriving ... they [jealous boyfriends or crazed fans] would all be there, trying to shoot the plane!"

OK, I'm not asking you to make being an action hero one of your goals, but put this fab principle in perspective. Perhaps you've signed up for a glass-blowing class, but you discover it's to be held in a so-called bad part of town. Maybe your goal is to build your own dream house, but you realize you're fifteen pounds overweight and out of shape. Are you going to let these fears stop you before you start? Of course you're not! You're living the Beatles way!

The Risk Factor
"Baby take a chance with me . . ."
("Little Child," 1963)

It's simple: You take no risks, you get nowhere. The Beatles were willing to take huge risks in their career, and to show for it, they made huge strides in achievement, artistic accomplishment, and in fulfilling their wildest dreams. Paul explained, "There's risk in just going out in the morning. It'd be easier to just stay at home and send out videos [as promotions for his new music projects]. But that's not what I'm here for. This is life, the *main event*. I'd rather just get out and run the risk, than stay at home and rest on my laurels."

Not all risks involve taking action. Sometimes the risk is in saying no. In 1964, the Beatles turned down a sure chance for a feature rock 'n' roll film in Britain, *The Yellow Teddy Bears*. "It turned out that either somebody else would write the music, and we had to perform their songs," explained Paul, "and part of the deal also meant that we had to give away the copyright to any new songs that were featured in the film. We immediately decided that was too much, and we turned that offer down and waited until something better would turn up." Their instincts were right on. That "something better" turned out to be *A Hard Day's Night*.

And how's this for risk? In 1966, still selling out stadiums in the United States and even bigger venues throughout the rest of the world, the group agreed to stop touring and playing live. This was tantamount to commercial suicide. But again the Beatles trusted their instincts. The recording work they produced directly after that last tour—beginning with *Revolver* and quickly moving to "Strawberry Fields," "Penny Lane," and *Sgt. Pepper's Lonely Hearts Club Band*—makes it clear that the time spent *not* touring was being used in magnificently progressive—and commercial—ways.

One huge risk the Beatles took during their heyday was an unprecedented one—to leave their name completely *off* the cover of several of their albums. The Fabs knew their fans would find their new records without having to make the obvious pronouncements usually undertaken by the industry. This caused considerable consternation to their record company, and rightly so, as the omission may have confused fans and distributors. The Fabs began this trend by deploying the tiny title *Beatles for Sale* on the cover of their fourth U.K. album and wiping the Beatles name completely off the covers of *Rubber Soul, Revolver, Abbey Road*, and *Let It Be*. The *White Album* was even more radical: pure nothingness—only their name delicately embossed on the front. Think about this: Would you leave your name off your own product?

Embracing risk continued well into the Beatles' solo careers as well. Paul said that risk was behind the first project of his post-Beatles group, Wings. "We went off on a little university tour, which was very 'ballsy' to do. I didn't want to get together a big famous group, which the others had done. That felt just too safe for me. I felt like 'I got to risk it a bit more.'"

Risk. How does that word affect you? Do you often take the first thing offered to you on a new job hunt, even if intuitively it feels quite wrong? Think hard about this. When you graduated college, you might have taken the first job you came across, and now it's become your *career*. For the Beatles, simply saying "Thanks, but no thanks" was common for them. They had fixed goals in their agenda—goals they were willing to wait for, ones that were truly in line with their overall dream.

Work Is Fun!
"Gonna have some fun tonight..."
("Long Tall Sally," 1963)

All this attitude stuff sounds quite serious. Let's take a look at the flip side of the Beatles' rise. Many people view work, even in their chosen career, as a drag, a grind, a bore—something to do to pay bills or, worse, to distract oneself from thinking about unfulfilled dreams.

Not so for the Beatles. Being fab means *work is fun*! Here's John answering a question on this topic in 1971:

Question: "When did you realize that you were bigger than Elvis?"
John: "I don't know. You see, it's different once it happens. It's like, when you actually get to number one, it's different. It's the going for it that's the fun."

Regarding the writing of "She Loves You," Paul remembered, "John and I wrote that one in a hotel room on an afternoon off. God bless their little cotton socks, those boys worked! They worked their little asses off! Here I am talking about an afternoon off and we're sitting there writing! We just *loved it so much*, it wasn't work!"

And here's Paul on the stringent demands of Beatlemania: "It didn't seem like pressure. It was, but I don't remember it being a pressure. It was *fun*." Paul outlined this Beatle *work is fun* philosophy: "We don't look upon it as a business. It's a hobby more than anything."

The Beatles way means that you dream big and work hard at what you love. It means success—the kind of success that allows you, when it's no longer fun, to say good-bye. Paul summed it up: "By the time we got to Candlestick Park [in San Francisco to play their final 1966 concert], we knew that this just wasn't fun anymore." They moved on. If you live your life the Beatles way, you'll have that option too.

Saying "No, thanks" is something to think long and hard about. Do you spend enough time doing what you love? Can you figure out a way to make a living at it? That's the Beatles way. They used *fun* as a true barometer for their work. If they enjoyed it fully, they continued working on a project; however, if it got boring or became a grind, they'd immediately go off in a different direction. What's the barometer of your life—duty, predictability, or fun?

Truth in Arrogance
"Try to see it my way..."
("We Can Work It Out," 1965)

Let's look closely at a subject that rubs most people the wrong way but remains an essential component of being fab. And it's this: There is *truth in arrogance*. Let's review four comments, one from each Beatle.

Ringo: "I have nothing to prove any more, you know. *I am* the best rock 'n' roll drummer in the world."

Paul: "What you don't realize, is that we've *always* been at the top of heap. When we started out in Liverpool, or playing in Hamburg, or at no matter what level, we were at the top. At each level we've always been at the top, so this is really nothing new for us."

George: "We just had this amazing inner feeling of 'We're going to *do it*!' We were just cocky."

John: "When I was a Beatle, I thought we were the best fucking group in the goddamn world, and *believing* that is what made us what we were."

Wow! Cocky blokes indeed. Of course, you've got to have the "chops" to back up such grandiose statements, which of course they did. But let's reflect on this topic of arrogance just a bit further.

Most civilized people agree that a large degree of humility is admirable, especially from people who are doing well in life. And granted, the Beatles had their fair share of it. They were self-proclaimed "lucky guys," "blessed with talent and fame." Even John wrote "I'm a Loser" at the height of Beatlemania. But the truth is that they knew they were talented and that they alone were responsible for their chosen dreams and ensuing destinies.

"I sometimes hear myself in interviews going: 'Well, I'm just a sort of ordinary guy,'" said Paul, adding, "But I think, 'Will they go away thinking, "Did he really say he was an ordinary guy?"' Because there's a lot of evidence to the contrary. We knew we were *good*. People used to ask us, 'Are you conceited?' It's a difficult question, because I'd have to answer yes, because I think we are good, but that thought actually amounts to conceit, doesn't it? But I'd be stupid to say we weren't good, because it's so obvious that Beatle music is good stuff, and it's number one everywhere, so somebody's buying it."

And there's nothing wrong with the arrogance that comes from being a proud competitor. Paul put his confidence right on the table: "I'd put me at the top. Just because I'm a competitor man! You've got to slog man, I've slogged my way from the suburbs of Liverpool, and I am not about to put all that down."

"Well, who else is there? We were the monsters!" agreed Ringo. "There's been a lot of biggies, and very few monsters. That's the difference."

John, as usual, got to the point: "If being an egomaniac means I believe in what I do, and in my art or my music, then in that respect you can call me that. I believe in what I do and I'll say that."

And in a 1971 *Rolling Stone* interview, when asked if he thought he was a genius, John revealed his feelings about his talents: "Yes, if there is such a thing as one, I am one. People like me are aware of their so-called genius at ten, eight, nine. I always wondered, 'Why has nobody discovered me?' In school, didn't they see that I'm cleverer than anybody in that school? That the teachers are stupid, too? That all they had was information that I didn't need? I got fuckin' lost in being at high school. I used to say to me auntie, 'You throw my fuckin' poetry out, and you'll regret it when I'm famous,' and she threw the bastard stuff out. I never forgave her for not treating me like a fuckin' genius or whatever I was, when I was a child. It was obvious to me."

Come on, own up! I'll bet you five bucks you wouldn't have the nerve to say something even remotely resembling the comments from the Fabs—including Ringo—about *yourself*. And that's a shame, because you do know maybe deep deep down that you're good—maybe even great— at certain things in your life. How about motherhood? How about garden- ing? How about being a responsive friend? But if asked about it, I bet you say, "Aw shucks, me? I'm just lucky."

OK, maybe I'm being a bit rough on you concerning this point of going public with your self-proclaimed genius. So how about this? Will you at least look in the mirror and tell yourself how great you are? Come on! Do it! You *are* great! The mirror awaits.

Reject Rejection
"Don't Bother Me"
(*With the Beatles*, 1963)

Let's get into another fab attitude that spurred the group onward—and that's the ability to *reject rejection*. When you're working at your dreams, criticism and rejection are a fact of life. As the Beatles found, you've got to literally *reject rejection* or you'll never get a dream one foot off the ground.

Early on, as dreaming teens, John and Paul heard endless rejections, even from those closest to them. John's aunt, Mimi Smith, who raised him, said, "To me [John's music] was just so much of a waste of time. I used to tell him so." She often said to him, "The guitar's all very well, John, but you'll never make a living out of it." Paul heard this from his father again and again as well. "He wanted me to have a career more than anything. 'It's all very well to play in a group,' he'd say, 'but you'll have to have a trade to fall back on.'"

And of course, during Brian Epstein's attempt at securing the Beatles a record deal in 1962, time and again he had to report back to the "boys" that he had been rejected. One infamous comment from a Decca executive still resounds in Beatle lore: "Go back to Liverpool, Mr. Epstein. Groups with guitars are out."

Even after four hit singles in the United Kingdom, Capitol Records refused to release Beatles records in the United States. Its senior executive in New York, Alan Livingston, maintained that Capitol didn't think the Beatles would "do anything" in the American market. Another executive offered Livingston his expert advice: "They're a bunch of long-haired kids. They're *nothing.*" Wow! *Nothing?*

Accordingly, the Beatles were forced to release their British mega-hits in the United States on the tiny Chicago R&B label Vee Jay Records. And after the Beatles had scored their third consecutive number-one single in Britain, neither Capitol—nor Vee Jay, by now—thought the Beatles had any prospects in America, so "She Loves You" was relegated to an even smaller New York–based label, Swan Records. Not until November 1963, when worldwide press coverage was too much to ignore and Brian Epstein had personally hand-carried a copy of their next U.K. number-one record to Capitol, did it agree to release a Beatles record in America. That record was "I Want to Hold Your Hand."

In reviews published at the time, critics were not kind to the Beatles. *Time* magazine called *A Hard Day's Night* "rubbish which should be avoided at all costs." And *Newsweek* pronounced in February 1964, "Musically, the Beatles are a near-disaster: guitars slamming out a merciless beat that does away with secondary rhythms, harmony, and melody. Their lyrics, punctuated by nutty shouts of 'yeah yeah yeah!,' are a catastrophe, a preposterous farrago of Valentine-card romantic sentiments." Fighting words such as these might have quelled the spirit of a less confident group.

And a March 1964 *Saturday Evening Post* article said of the longevity of Beatlemania, "Crazes tend to die a horribly abrupt death. It was not so long ago, after all, that a good many unwary businessmen got caught with warehouses full of coonskin caps when the Davy Crockett craze stopped almost without warning."

Overall, the media mercilessly manhandled the Beatles in both the United States and the United Kingdom. There were endless negative questions at press conferences, with reporters trying to push the group into controversy or to uncover some "secret scandal." Questions focused on why local governments were spending "so much money" on security or why fans had been hurt in so-called "stampedes."

Often the press would try to goad the Beatles with questions on why there were "hoards of protestors" outside their hotels or concerts, though in actual fact, these "hoards" consisted of a mere handful of jealous boyfriends and the like.

How did the Beatles handle all this? By knowing who was important—the fans—and knowing who could be dismissed. Check out Paul's confident attitude in 1967 toward the soon-to-be released *Sgt. Pepper*: "Many of the newspapers had been saying a month before, 'What are the Beatles up to?' and 'Are the Beatles drying up?' Well, it was lovely to have that on them." Paul *knew* that what the Beatles were developing with the *Pepper* record was special, even revolutionary.

Paul noted that criticism and rejection were not factors in how he or the Beatles measured their talent. "*Sales* is the best indicator. That's why I always feel it's funny when people say, 'Oh, it doesn't matter whether it sells, you don't look at that aspect.' I think that's what *does* matter, the people out there with their little pennies, going to the shop and spending them. I think it's a big move, to spend your money on someone. Some people think that's just commercialism, but I think it's the public vote."

So many of us are intimidated by what others *might* say—or *might* think about our dreams—that we don't even get our dreams off the ground. Fear of rejection is a major obstacle in the goal process.

Do you have the inner knowingness to withstand the negativity that will surely ensue once you get your dream into reality mode?

Expect Success
"All I've Got to Do"
(*With the Beatles*, 1963)

There's one further element to an attitude that's fab: *Expect success*.

In 1971, John discussed their expectations when the Beatles first came to the United States. "We were really professional by the time we got here [to the United States]. We had learned the whole game. When we arrived, we knew how to handle the press. The British press are the toughest in the world; so we could handle anything. I know on the plane over, I was saying, 'Oh, we won't make it,' or I said that on a film or something, but that's that side of me.... [But] we *knew* we would wipe you out if we could just get a grip on you."

Paul saw the States as just another land to conquer: "America was the greatest 'show-biz town,' and we were just very confident. Our confidence was at an all-time high." And Ringo agreed: "It was sort of an attitude we had. We'd conquered England, Sweden, and we conquered France. America was *ours* now."

The recording studio was also a place in which the Fabs expected success. One notable example occurred during the recording of "Strawberry Fields Forever," done in several different takes. One of them, take seven, was a contemplative ballad version, and another, take twenty-six, was a heavier, faster, orchestral version. The challenge? John liked the first part of the slow one—and the second part of the fast one.

George Martin relayed the story: "John said to me, 'I like them both. Why don't we put them together? You could start with take seven and move to take twenty-six halfway through to get the grandstand finish!' 'Brilliant!' I replied, sarcastically. 'There are only two things wrong with that: the takes are in completely different keys, a whole tone apart, and they have wildly different tempos. Other than that, there should be no problem!' John smiled at my sarcasm with the tolerance of a grown-up placating a child. 'Well, George,' he said laconically, 'I'm sure you can fix it, can't you?' whereupon he turned on his heel and walked away!"

Indeed, John's faith in expecting success motivated Martin to accommodate John's request with brilliant inventiveness. He sped up the slower take seven and slowed down the faster take twenty-six, which enabled the keys and tempos to match, and then spliced the two together in the middle. If you listen closely to "Strawberry Fields Forever," you can clearly hear this edit at exactly sixty seconds into the song.

Success. Failure. Which do you expect on your journey to your dreams? For the Beatles, success at every turn was to be expected. Their dreams were realized well before the actualization of them living it. As Sun Tzu wrote in the two-thousand-year-old classic *The Art of War*, "Before doing battle, in the temple [of the mind] one calculates and will win." The Beatles followed that advice to the letter. They knew they'd conquered America before they even arrived in New York City.

How do you stack up in this principle? Think of a situation where you came off well. Perhaps before a job interview you felt strong, capable, and ideal for the slot. And you did get the job. How can that attitude enable you in attaining the goals it will take for you to achieve your dream?

Don't Take Your Dream Too Seriously

"You can't cry 'cause you're laughing at me..."
("I'm Down," 1965)

"That was part of the thing," George said, "the Beatles were very funny. I mean they actually were funny."

The four intensely scrutinized Beatles had a secret code, which they used often to protect themselves and to deflate the tension of the Beatlemania raging around them. "It was an ability with words," remarked Paul on the subject. "It became one of the Beatles' specialties. You know, where producer George Martin would say, 'Anything you don't like?' and George Harrison would say, 'We don't like your tie.' As kids on the street, we just called it 'wisecracks.'"

George blurted out another wisecrack to cut the tension during the group's first official meeting with Brian Epstein. John, George, and Pete Best had already arrived. But there was no sign of Paul. Brian was becoming irritated and asked George to ring Paul up on the phone. George returned from the phone to say that Paul was in the bath. "This is disgraceful," said a rattled Brian. "He's going to be very late." "Late," said George, in his classic deadpan manner, "but very clean."

Paul discussed the effect of humor within the band: "That was one of the great things about John," he said, speaking about the group's first Shea Stadium concert in 1965 in front of fifty-seven thousand screaming fans. "If ever there was a tense show, which that one actually was, John's comedy would come in. He'd start with the [pulling] faces, and his shoulders would start going. It was very encouraging to us, and we'd go, 'Oh, that's good, at least we're not taking it seriously!'"

Humor also entered into their unique brand of self-marketing as well. For instance, after naming their business "Apple," they went one better with the name, not merely calling it Apple Limited or Apple Corporation. Rather, the humorous "Apple Corps Ltd." was the final choice.

Let's finish off this topic with a little-known question-and-answer during a Los Angeles press conference in August 1966, in which a reporter was digging to find something nasty to write about the group.

Question: "I'd like to direct this question to Messieurs Lennon and McCartney. In a recent article, *Time* magazine recently put down pop music, and they referred to 'Day Tripper' as being about a prostitute."
Paul (nodding jokingly): "Oh yeah."
Question: "And 'Norwegian Wood' as being about a lesbian."
Paul (nodding): "Oh yeah."
Question: "I just wanted to know what your intent was when you wrote those songs, and what your feeling is about the *Time* magazine criticism of the music that is being written today?"
Paul: "We were just trying to write songs about prostitutes and lesbians, that's all." (*Room erupts with laughter and applause.*)

Though often taken for granted, humor is integral to the Beatles way. They rarely took themselves seriously publicly, especially in the early days. Even later, during serious antiwar events such as John and Yoko's "Bed-Ins for Peace," John was happy to be a self-proclaimed "fool for peace." They knew the power of laughter to put themselves and others at ease. In their movies, many critics hailed the group as "the new Marx Brothers."

How often do you employ humor in going for your goals? Here's an idea to warm up your humor muscle. Examine a tough or sensitive situation you're anticipating in the near future. Thinking of asking your boss for a raise? Instead of going the serious route and listing your accomplishments, what about disarming your boss? Have a balloon made up that reads, "I'm worth it!"

The next time an argument with your spouse is about to begin, why not diffuse the situation with something funny? Rent a clown costume and come out doing a tap dance. John said it best in 1965: "Life is very short, and there's no time for fussing and fighting, my friend."

YOU'RE THE FIFTH BEATLE! — *Attitude*

★ What's your attitude about the *unknown*? Does the word terrify you— or excite you? It's clear from the Beatles that they welcomed it. John said, "Accept that it's all unknown and it's plain sailing." What's making you fearful of the unknown? What stops you from making a positive move toward achieving your dreams? Think about the song "All You Need Is Love" and pretend you're singing it "live" to an audience of 400 million people! The Beatles did exactly that, without flinching. Could you? From practicing this, you'll get the sense of exactly how much power lies within simple confidence.

★ Emotions are so powerful that they literally fuel us through every waking moment, adding excitement to our lives. However, in being fab, you'll need to effectively detach yourself from emotion in order to turn your dreams into reality. The bigger the dream, the more detachment needed. Practice *not* having emotional feelings during a task you normally dread. For instance, go up to a person you admire and tell him or her so. Don't hold back. Think up ways to actively address an emotional situation, and then confront it without having an emotion. When a conflict arises, try to steady yourself to the point where you are simply observing the scene—even your own reactions. By doing this, your clearheadedness will bring at least one logical set of solutions—yours!—to the fore.

★ The Beatles took huge risks in their career, but along the way, they achieved continual artistic milestones and lived out bigger and bigger dreams. What kind of risk could you take right now that would further your wildest dream? If your dream entails buying a new state-of-the-art computer system and scanner, maybe it's time to dip into your savings and purchase them. The amount of confidence you have in yourself and your abilities will determine the actual risk. If you know you're ready and able, then taking action should not even be considered a "risk." Go even riskier. Is it time to refinance your house to get the money you'll need to finance your dream? Careful—the more it feels to you a risk, the more it probably is. It should feel doable, natural, and right before taking any such action. If you ran the risk of trying for a dream, what would happen? Would it necessarily be negative? Perhaps it's only your perception that something negative would happen. The reality might actually be a joyous experience.

★ Here's a tough one. For the Beatles, there was a real truth and a freedom in being arrogant. Is that word anathema to you? Do you continually need to tell people around you that you "don't deserve" to be successful? Do you feel the need to say "I'm just lucky" if you have a degree of success? Don't forget what John liked to say about his group: "When I was a Beatle, I thought we were the best fucking group in the goddamn world, and *believing* that is what made us what we were." Take a few moments and write down what's truly *incredible* about *you*! Get the sense of your own self-worth, and practice bringing that attitude out in public.

★ Here's a fun exercise designed to uncover your humorous side. Rent *A Hard Day's Night*, preferably a few times. Rediscover the wit and slapstick the group deploys throughout the movie. Ask yourself: How can I use humor to relax myself and to disarm the people around me and the world at large in a positive manner?

4 TEAM

The fact is we were a team,
despite everything
that went on between us and around us.

—Paul McCartney

You're doing great—you're well on your way to being a Fifth Beatle. As the Beatles themselves would say, "Gear, mate! Fab, luv!" You've been dreaming; you've been doing your sketches; you've set yourself some realistic goals; and you're developing a Beatle-like attitude about success and raising your expectations to receive it.

However, being fab is not something you can be alone, so here's where we move on to the next critical element in the Beatles way: *creating and maintaining a team*, one that will take you all the way to your dreams.

In this chapter, we'll look not only at developing a qualified and loyal team but also at choosing a leader, sacrificing for the greater good of the team, and sharpening a competitive spirit that will give you the edge you need.

Leadership
"I'll Follow the Sun"
(*Beatles for Sale*, 1964)

The first thing any team needs is a leader. John Lennon was the de facto leader of the Beatles through their fledgling early days and right up until the end of Beatlemania in 1966, when Paul McCartney was the man in command.

Paul is quite forward with his praise of John. In 1991 he said, "Looking back on it with John, I always idolized him. We all did, the group. I don't know if the others will tell you that, but he was our idol." Paul also said, even earlier, "We all looked up to John, he was older and he was very much the leader; he was the quickest wit, and the smartest."

Ringo agreed, saying about John in the early '60s, "He was like our own little Elvis. Very forceful, very funny, very bright, and always someone for us to look up to."

It's obvious from his sheer charisma, talent, and wit why the Beatles tended to gravitate around John for leadership, but Paul provided for a deeper psychological insight into the nature of leadership: "Actually I've always quite enjoyed being second. I realized why that was when I was horseback riding recently—that whoever is first opens all the gates. If you're second, you get to just walk through, they've knocked down all the walls, all the stinging nettles . . . you're still up with number one. Number one still needs you as his companion. I think my relationship to John is something to do with this attitude."

Nonetheless, when the time came for Paul to lead, he did so, and brilliantly.

First off, Paul spearheaded the making of *Sgt. Pepper's Lonely Hearts Club Band*, and then he pushed the group to make the underrated *Magical Mystery Tour* and *Let It Be* films and their accompanying soundtrack albums. Paul also roused the Beatles from their meditative state under Maharishi Mahesh Yogi to pull together the *White Album* and brought them together to go out with the huge bang called *Abbey Road*. He was also instrumental in their business start-up, Apple Corps Ltd.

So which are you—follower or leader? If your dream is a hefty one, involving a group of people—even two or three—you've no choice but to lead that team. And who better to emulate than John? He had the ability to lead without dominating. You've heard the Beatles discuss John in glowing terms, almost as if he didn't actually lead them at all but rather engaged them at a level where they were willing to follow him without question. How? He had earned their trust.

How do you measure up in the trust department? Do your friends and family completely trust you? Would they speak of you as the Beatles spoke of John? Are you impeccable in your words and actions toward them? Do you have their best interests at heart, or merely your own?

Situations involving trust will pop up often in your life, especially if you're conscious of them. Think about it: If a cashier gives you back too much change, what do you do? Do you give it back, or do you pocket it and quickly walk out of the store? If a co-worker has come up with a great idea on how to streamline production, how do you handle it? Do you take the credit for it, or do you champion that person's idea with the greater good of the team in mind? Look at your relationship with your spouse or your children. Are your words impeccable? Do you practice what you preach, or do you often say one thing and do another?

Encouraging Your Team

"Don't you know it's going to be alright..."
("Revolution," 1969)

Being fab takes attitude even to the point of arrogance. That said, one sign of a great leader is the ability to surrender yourself to others with great talent. John's arrogance didn't get in the way of recognizing the genius of others. At the ripe old age of sixteen, John knew that the younger Paul was an obvious threat in many aspects—talent, looks, showmanship—but even then John had the instincts of a great leader. "I had a mutual friend who brought Paul to see my group, the Quarrymen. I saw he had talent.

Since I was the leader, I had to make the decision: Was it better to have a guy who was better than the people I had in the group, or not? And that decision was to let Paul in, to make the group stronger."

Directly after this decision that would change their fates, John noted, "Paul then introduced me to George, and I had to make [another] decision—whether or not to let George in the group. I listened to George play and I let him in. Then the rest of the [Quarrymen] group was gradually thrown out. Instead of going for the individual thing, we went for the strongest format—for equals."

Look at the impact that the decision of "letting George in" had on the Beatles. George's prowess shines through on intricate lead guitar parts in "She Loves You" and "Help!" and it evolved into his slide guitar stylings on songs from "Come Together" to "My Sweet Lord," influencing guitarists worldwide. His songwriting on such classics as "Taxman," "While My Guitar Gently Weeps," and "Something" gave the world some of the best and most acclaimed Beatle songs ever. And George's Hindu conversion and related Indian musical influences ultimately brought that culture to the attention of a huge percentage of the Western populace. George's vocal-harmony abilities, wry humor, intuitive intelligence, and quiet strength helped carry the group to heights that might have remained unattainable without him.

In 1968, John summed up the incredible benefit that came of making these integral decisions in picking his first real team: "Now there were three of us who thought the same."

You can see the core Beatles team coming together here, due largely to John making the decision to expand his team with equals rather than subordinates. Think about what might have happened to John had he not had the foresight and humbleness to accept Paul and George. It's highly doubtful that his original group, the Quarrymen, would have had much of an impact outside the Liverpool region.

Yet once John had his team of equals, he didn't hesitate to assert his control as leader. "How do you describe the job [of being a leader]? I maneuver people, that's what leaders do. I sit and make situations which will be of benefit to me and other people. It's as simple as that." He added, "Maneuvering is what is, let's not be coy about it. It's a deliberate and thought-out maneuver of how to get a situation how I want it."

Think about John's leadership quality in relation to yourself. Would you have the nerve to allow someone on your team who's as talented as you are? Perhaps you feel protective of your dream and would prefer not to let others be involved as integrally as you. Yet think about John's decision-making process. Would you have his fab wisdom in allowing a talent as formidable as Paul McCartney into your team? Contemplate the people who are on the short list to be on your team. Can you envision yourself being truthful with each person and allowing all their qualities to surface and shine? Imagine situations that will arise in going for your dream and project each prospective person into that situation. Will you bond, or will personal issues arise, such as jealousy, pettiness, or control issues? Fab wisdom says think deeply, clearly, and honestly about putting together an awesome team! Be arrogant, but be humble too!

Perfecting the Team
"They're gonna crucify me..."
("The Ballad of John and Yoko," 1969)

Looking closer at the Beatles' decision-making processes, you'll see another element in his methodology: a cold-eyed ability to trim the fat. Let's look at several decisions, the first involving the sacking of former band member Pete Best, who was replaced just as the Beatles were signing their first recording contract. The decision to fire Pete was not an easy one. At the time, the Beatles were the most popular act in Liverpool, with fans queuing up a full day before performances to secure tickets. Secondly, the other drummer they had in mind to replace Pete, Ringo Starr, was working full-time in another popular band, Rory Storm and the Hurricanes. It wasn't guaranteed that Ringo would leave his cushy spot with that group.

To complicate matters further, Pete was the de facto heartthrob in the group. His James Dean good looks and greaser hairdo held a huge attraction for the "birds" who flocked to see the group. So why did John, Paul, and George feel it necessary to replace him?

Well, to a professional musician's ear, it's clear that Pete's drumming is dragging the beat—not to any great degree, but just enough to keep at bay the sheer energy of the group, which is just *bursting* to move faster, harder, and louder.

And Pete wasn't getting with the program. Pictures of the group at the time show John, Paul, and George with a professional "suit and tie" look and with blow-dried haircuts, long and brushed down over their foreheads. It was a unified look—except for Pete, who is quite conspicuous with his greasy, old-school ducktail hairdo.

Paul said in 1967 to official biographer Hunter Davies, "I wasn't jealous of [Pete] because he was [more] handsome. That's all junk. He just couldn't play. Ringo was so much better. We wanted him out for that reason." George has said as much, and as the most meticulous of musicians, he was adamant that Pete had to go.

There were a few others who didn't make the cut as the Beatles' overarching dream began to manifest into reality, most notably Stuart Sutcliffe and Allan Williams. Sutcliffe, though a close friend of John's and an artist who helped the group move into unique directions with their image, was not strong enough as a musician to participate as the group began to become popular and the stakes grew higher. A similar situation occurred with their first official manager, Allan Williams. While at first he was able to get the Beatles their initial important concert dates in Hamburg, his importance leveled off as the group began to find better gigs for them-selves than he could. He was let go in 1961.

Cutting your losses is a hard but necessary part of the Beatles way. Look closely at how your goals are set up. Do you intuitively know that some part of your plan is weak or that perhaps there's a person involved in your goal-team who's holding you back? Is that the one person who's just not up to snuff talent-wise or energy-wise to effectively help you on the way to your dream? Do you have the nerve—as the Fabs did—to face the music and make some cold, hard changes?

For the Greater Good

"Try to see it my way..."
("We Can Work It Out," 1965)

Sometimes, to move your dream along, you've got to sacrifice your ego. The songwriting collaboration deal between John and Paul led to their being perhaps the most successful and influential songwriting team in his-tory. "When we started with the Lennon and McCartney thing, it was 50/50 with a handshake," said Paul, "it was like a Rodgers and Hammer-stein trip." He added, "That romantic image of collaboration, all those films about New York City songwriters plugging away at the piano, that always appealed to me, that image. Lennon and McCartney were to become the Rodgers and Hammerstein of the '60s; that's the way the dream went."

John underscored the point: "Paul and I made a deal when we were fifteen. There was never a legal deal between us, just a deal we made when we decided to write together, that we put both our names on it, no matter what." Well, you know "the rest is history" bit! But they sacrificed 50 percent of their royalties, which they never did renegotiate throughout their career—even though they had pretty much stopped collaborating during the Beatlemania days. Here's one clear example: It's well known that Paul was the sole writer of "Yesterday." But if you look at the credits, even on their recent *1* CD, the song credits "Lennon, McCartney." Well, now that's sacrifice!

And how's this for sacrifice for the greater good of a dream? Paul McCartney's first and preferred Beatle instrument was the guitar, not the bass. "None of us wanted to be the bass player [in 1961]," admitted Paul. "It wasn't the number-one job. We all wanted to be up front singing, looking good, to pull the birds."

But after the Beatles played their second season of gigs in Hamburg, Stu Sutcliffe announced he was going to stay in Hamburg. "So it was like 'Uh-oh, we haven't got a bass player,'" remembered Paul. "And everyone sort of turned and looked at me!" But take it on he did, and eventually Paul became one of the most innovative and respected bass players in rock history.

Later, at the height of Beatlemania, the Beatles sacrificed their hard-rock R&B image when the four decided that Paul's song "Yesterday" would be better off without their usual accompaniment. You can hear Paul teaching the song to the others on *Anthology II* as per their usual practice, but they soon decided that a simple string quartet and Paul's lone acoustic guitar would best suit the song musically. To play it somewhat on the safe side, the group didn't release the song as a single in Britain, perhaps to keep their reputation as a hard-core rock 'n' roll group intact. But with its release in the United States, the song went to number one, and today "Yesterday" is the most popular song of the group's canon.

Being fab means honing the ability to sacrifice your own limited interests to achieve even wilder successes. Don't underestimate the size and scope of your dream—it's possible that others on your dream-team could have hidden attributes that will help reap huge potential. They only need to be nurtured by you—and ultimately will benefit not only you and them but the world at large.

Give Praise Sparingly

"That when I tell you that I love you..."
("I Should Have Known Better," 1964)

The Beatles recorded a beautiful Buddy Holly song, "Words of Love," but one of John's leadership techniques was all about *not* actually saying many words of love. In fact, according to Paul, praise was in short supply from his mentor, John. True to their rather tough Liverpool upbringing, encouragement best remained unspoken. However, when John did give praise, always in private, it had a profound effect.

"Whenever John did praise any of us, it was great praise, indeed," said Paul, "because he didn't dish it out much. If ever you got a *speck* of it, a *crumb* of it, you were quite grateful. I remember one time when we were making *Help!* in Austria. We'd been out skiing all day for the film and we were all tired. I usually shared a room with George, but on this occasion, I was in with John. We were taking our huge skiing boots off and getting ready for the evening and stuff, and we had on one of our albums *Rubber Soul*, and for the first time ever, he just tossed it off, 'Oh, I probably like your songs better than mine.' And that was it! That was the height of praise I ever got off him. Whoops! There was no one looking, so he could say it!"

That kind of quiet and occasional encouraging of your team is worth a truckload of "attaboys" and overused phrases. John knew praise had to be spare, directed, and specific. Here's another example: At a Rock and Roll Hall of Fame induction, Paul remembered that John liked it when Paul imitated Little Richard on early Beatles hard-rocking numbers such as "Long Tall Sally."

"I remember doing the vocal to 'Kansas City,'" he said to John, in spirit. "Well, I couldn't quite get it, because it's hard to do that stuff you know, screaming out the top of your head. [But] you came down from the control room, took me to one side, and said, 'You can do it, you've just got to scream, you can do it!' So, thank you. Thank you for that. I did it!"

Ringo was never much on the receiving end of praise from either John or Paul, and often he had to turn to George for enthusiasm for his drumming or songwriting abilities. You can see that in the film *Let It Be* when George helps Ringo figure out a catchy chord progression on the piano for Ringo's charming work-in-progress "Octopus's Garden." But occasionally the others did pile on the praise for Ringo. In 1968, he was just plain fed up with the grueling, drawn-out sessions for the *White Album*. He felt he wasn't "fitting in" (his words) at the time, so he left.

The others quickly intervened. "We had to reassure him that we did think he was great," remembered Paul, "but that's what it's like in life, you go through life, and you never stop and say, 'Hey, you know what? I think you're great!'" Accordingly, George covered Ringo's drum kit completely in flowers, and John sent Ringo telegrams announcing, "You're the world's best rock drummer, come on home!" Ringo said of all the attention, "It was great, and then the *White Album* really took off. I just felt good about myself and we got through that crisis."

John Lennon hardly ever gave compliments, and for good reason. You can see by the other Beatles' comments that any morsel of praise from John was as good as gold. John's well-planned praise was a subtle motivational factor for the continued creativity of the group.

Listen hard to your own words of encouragement. Are you over the top in your approach? John wasn't. He expected excellence from his team. After all, he was giving it. Think about the members on your own team. Everyone has a different need for encouragement and praise. Some might need real hand-holding to enable themselves to give their all. Others might appreciate you trusting them to self-start and bring their own brand of genius to the table.

Loyalty

"As you are me / And we are all together..."
("I Am the Walrus," 1967)

Praise of your team is intimately connected with its unity, bonding, and loyalty. Let's take a peek at these terms in action from the Beatles. During a 1963 press conference, a unique and palpable camaraderie was evident among the Fabs:

Question: "Does the continuous living together and working together cause any temperamental stress on you?"
Paul: "No, actually it's quite lucky because we've been..."
Beatles (in unison): "We've been together now for forty yeeeears!" (*singing a then-popular song*).
Paul: "You know, we've all been mates for quite a long time, so we don't get on each other's nerves as much as we could." (*Mock-fighting breaks out between them.*)

And a press interview during their 1964 world tour revealed their remarkable unity:

Question: "You Beatles have conquered five continents. What would you like to do next?"
Beatles (in unison): "Conquer six!"

For the core Fab Four, the bond between them was consistent. Early childhood experiences figured into this bond, as they'd all grown up within a mile or two of each other; they had similar tastes in music, clothes, and women; they spoke the same wisecracking "scouse" language; and they had the same sharp, self-protective wit. Going deeper, both John and Paul had lost their mothers as teens: "We were both wounded animals," explained Paul, "and just looking at each other, we knew the pain we were feeling."

George said perceptively of the group's bond in 1964, "The thing is, none of us profess to be individually great musicians, nor very talented, but the thing is, as a group, I think we're good. I think we're much better as a group than we are individually."

This group bond solidified as John and Paul worked together on something as intimate as songwriting, letting their guards down, trying out new ideas, and baring their souls through their intensely personal lyrics. John said of those early days, "We wrote a lot of stuff together one-to-one, eyeball to eyeball. Like in 'I Want to Hold Your Hand,' I remember when we got the chord that made the song. We were in Jane Asher's house, downstairs in the cellar playing on the piano at the same time. And we had, 'Oh you, got that something…' And Paul hits this chord [a B minor chord], and I turned to him and said, 'That's it! Do *that* again!' In those days, we really used to absolutely write like that, both playing into each other's noses." Paul agreed wholeheartedly: "'Eyeball to eyeball' is a very good description of it. That's exactly how it was!"

This bonding trickled down through the group as a whole. George said in 1964, "I've been with John and Paul for more than six years now, and we know each other inside out. Our individual characteristics, and I include Ringo in this, balance against one another remarkably well." He added, "It's because our personalities work at different pressures that we get on so well together as a team." Ringo concurred, "The best thing about this group is that we all work everything out between us. It doesn't matter who is playing what. If someone thinks of something, then we'll try it.

If I'm playing the drums and someone says, 'Try this here, or do some-thing there,' I'll try it. It's the same with all of us."

Paul relayed how this unity figured so predominately in the early suc-cess of the group when it came to choosing songs to record and perform: "Each one of them made it through the Beatles test. We all had to like it. If anyone didn't like one of our songs, it was vetoed. It could be vetoed by one person. If Ringo said, 'I don't like that one,' we wouldn't do it, or we'd have to really persuade him."

John discussed this intimate bond in 1967 with this uncharacteristi-cally loving statement: "If I'm on my own for three days, doing nothing, I almost completely leave myself. I'm at the back of my head. I can see my hands and realize they're moving, but it's like a robot who's doing it. I have to see the others to see myself."

George summed it up: "We always had that confidence [in unity]. That was the good thing about being four together, unlike Elvis. I always felt sorry for Elvis because he was on his own. He had his guys with him, but there was only one Elvis, but nobody else knew what he felt like. For us, we all shared the experience."

With your own team, don't let unity and loyalty be mere words. Are you actively promoting the involvement of everyone on your team? The Beatles all worked on every facet of their act (except for songwriting) and they shared ideas equally in the recording studio, in live performances, and in creating their image. Consider the teams you're part of in your own life. Are your family meetings open to everyone's input? How about your business deal-ings? At the Monday meeting, is one person calling the shots? Fab wisdom means creating democratic and pleasurable projects for all to participate in.

Being fab also means bonding. It's time for you to do as the Beatles did and share openly—and often—with your dream-team. The Beatles lived out of each other's suitcases, literally. You needn't go that far; however, you might consider hanging more often with your team outside of the actual business of accomplishing your dream. Dinners, parties, informal chats—consider fun, non-goal-oriented activities such as these to bond deeper with your team. Even better are party games like charades and truth or dare to help a team discover each other on a more personal level.

Engaging Your Team
"If I fell in love with you…"
("If I Fell," 1964)

Whether for small dreams or for really big Beatle-style dreams, one thing you'll need is a team that you engage with your talent, enthusiasm, and honesty. You might be able to *force* people to work for you, but unless your strategy includes the kind of long-term devotion that the Fabs attracted, Beatle-size success is unlikely to be yours.

It was indeed the core Fabs who were the central team force; however, they created a magnificent circle of people whom they could trust—and who trusted them. And these people loved them with a rare respect and devotion. None of them were necessarily technically qualified for their jobs either, just as none of the Beatles were schooled in music. Their simple qualities of honesty, integrity, and loyalty were the main ingredients in why these relationships worked.

Let's look at the premier person the Fabs engaged to work for them—and who ultimately may have literally died for them. Young Brian Epstein, who ran a record-store chain in Britain, was looking to do something exciting in his life, something big. He was twenty-seven years old in 1962 and fell for the group so hard that he gave them his near-undivided attention for five years until his death at age thirty-two.

Brian's trust and loyalty were so complete that he never even signed his name on the initial management contract with them. He was that respectful of their talent. He believed that if he couldn't help them, there would be no need for a legally binding agreement. Brian said, "I had given my word about what I intended to do and that was enough. I abided by the terms and no one ever worried about me not signing it." In this day of litigious consciousness, this would be unheard of, but ask yourself, why should that be so? If you and your team are honest and have respect for each other, contracts are superfluous.

Pete Best, then the drummer for the group, said later about this unique and artistic man, "The thing with Brian was that he made it quite clear when we went up to see him. He said, 'I have no musical knowledge, nor do I know very much about show business or the record business.' He was genuine. He simply said, 'I'll be prepared to do what I can.' And we accepted him for that."

So the lesson is this: You can teach almost anyone a skill, but what you can't teach are integrity and loyalty.

Look at the love and belief that Brian had for his beloved "boys," as he was fond of calling them. There's the famed story of his reaction to George Martin during an audition of the Beatles for Martin's record label. "When the demo was finished [the Decca audition tape that Brian had been hawking around London]," Martin said, "I switched off the machine and looked at Brian. 'It's not great,' I said. While I dithered, Brian launched into his sales pitch, praising the Beatles to the skies, 'One day,' he told me, with a fanatical glitter in his eye, 'they'll be bigger than Elvis Presley!'" His loyalty was not misplaced.

The second major person in the Beatles' inner circle was the talented record producer George Martin. He complemented them perfectly in his breadth of knowledge in classical as well as pop music. His contributions had an extra dimension because of his experience in the humor market. He had produced several records of the Beatles' favorite comedy acts, Peter Sellers and the "Goon Show" troupe. Due to this eclectic approach to record-making, George Martin was considered a bit of a maverick at

EMI, for which he ran the Parlophone subsidiary label. His antiestablish-ment reputation certainly appealed to the young rock 'n' rollers.

George Martin must have known that the group had already been turned down by every record company in London in 1962, including EMI. Fortunately for the group, he had an intuitive sense about what makes a success. He knew something was special, unique, and compelling about the Beatles, something worth taking a chance on. Martin discussed the moment when he knew how to market his newly signed act: "I asked them to play 'Love Me Do.' Although Lennon and McCartney had writ-ten it together, I had asked Paul to sing lead, because I wanted John's har-monica part to bleed into the vocals. He obviously couldn't sing and play at the same time." He added, "So Paul was warbling away, and John was backing him with that peculiarly distinctive, nasal almost flat second har-mony that was to become a trademark of their early sound. And it sud-denly hit me right between the eyes! This was a *group* I was listening to. I should take them as a group. That distinctive harmony, and that unique blend of sound, *that* was the selling point!"

Martin, like Brian Epstein, was not immune to the Beatles' humor and intelligence. He often liked to say he was "won over by their charm." And as we've seen throughout this book, the four's enthusiasm for their work and their utter willingness to work hard were also big factors in George Martin's own willingness to commit his talents to working with them.

"I never made any money out of the Beatles' successes," said Martin, adding, "I just got my same EMI salary, as I was under contract. No one could say I rode on the back of the Beatles." In fact, in 1964, after thirty-seven weeks at number one with the Beatles and other acts he produced, his salary was begrudgingly raised by EMI to a mere 3,200 pounds a year. Still, he stuck with the Beatles until they disbanded, and he even worked with them during their solo careers and on the newer Beatle projects such as the *Anthology* series.

Brian Epstein as manager and George Martin as music producer were huge components in taking the Fab Four to the zenith of worldwide success. Remember, you have to have your own act together before you can attract great people around you to join you in your dream's journey. Traits like humor, charm, class, hard work, dedication, and loyalty come up again and again when the Beatles are described. Sure, genius was involved, but genius goes unnoticed if it's not just one piece of the overall picture. Take a moment and think how these traits—both in yourself and in the people on your team—are vital to you on your own journey.

The Inner Circle

"Now I'll never dance with another..."
("I Saw Her Standing There," 1963)

Let's look closely at a few others who were in the inner circle, people whom the Fabs counted on everyday. We'll see why they trusted these folks, literally, with their lives.

First and foremost is Neil Aspinall. Neil was a close friend to Pete Best (the Fab's drummer before Ringo) during the early days of the group, went to the same school as Paul, and knew George as a young teen in Liverpool. By the time the Beatles were getting their stage legs, Neil made a major life change, leaving college where he was studying for a degree in accounting, to work full time for the group. Neil began his Beatle duties by getting the group local bookings and writing the posters for those early shows. During the Beatlemania days, Neil graduated from driver and roadie to tour coordinator on the group's world treks. Today, he is the chief executive at Apple Corps Ltd.

"I met Neil when I was thirteen years old," said George Harrison. "[We were] smoking behind the air-raid shelters at the Liverpool Institute high school. He's lasted forty years with the Beatles. Neil is the only person who's ever really been able to keep in contact with the four of us at the same time."

Working with Neil and the Fabs was Mal Evans, who also took a turn as van driver and roadie for the group early on. Mal quickly became enamored of the Beatles, having seen the group perform at the local Cavern Club. So smitten was he that—at age twenty-seven, married with a child, mortgage, and a job as a telecommunications engineer—Mal quit his secure job to hit the road with the group. He worked closely with them until the group's breakup in 1970.

Finally, we have Alf Bicknell, the Beatles' driver and road manager from 1964 to 1966, the group's touring years. Alf was devoted to the Beatles. One night, the Beatles were living one of their dreams—meeting Elvis Presley in his California home. Observing the large staff that attended to Elvis and his every whim, Alf leaned over to Ringo and said, "You know I've been thinking, Ringo. Elvis is just one guy, and he has about a dozen folks looking after him. Yet, there's four of you and only three of us [Neil, Mal, and Alf]." Ringo looked over and deadpanned, "What's the matter, Alf, you want a raise?"

Joking aside, you can clearly see how the Beatles, even deep into their mammoth popularity, relied on the smallest of personal staffs. The work must have been herculean for those three people, but these men shared the Beatles' dream, were inspired by the group's integrity, and were exhilarated by their work. Those are the hallmarks of a great team.

Who in your own life could muster up these selfless character traits in helping realize your dreams? Perhaps it's a childhood friend or relation you've known for many years. This kind of person will be an integral player on your dream-team, and most likely you will not be able to merely hire someone like that.

One more person epitomizes the perfect teammate: Derek Taylor, who left his promising job as a writer for a U.K. newspaper to work with the group he adored. He began as their press agent, reporting directly to Brian Epstein, and was himself a fellow Liverpudlian. Listen to his unabashed love for the group, spoken not long before he died in 1997: "The Beatles. Those faces, that time, that music. Some people say, it really was [about] the music, but that was only part of it. I joined because I wanted to be transported away from the world I've always known. They represented hope, optimism, wit, and lack of pretension, that 'anyone can do it' provided they had a will to do it. They seemed unstoppable!"

The Beatles inspired others to leave their jobs and follow them. They did more than create a body of work. They created a *feeling*. That's your job when you have a goal for your team. The Beatles relied on less than a handful of people in helping them to achieve their goals. In this day and age of specialists, this reliance on a select few "jacks-of-all-trades" seems like an idea whose time has come and gone. But think about the people you're considering to help you achieve your dream. Could one of them be capable of *several* of the tasks your goals require? So what if it takes some on-the-job training? Wouldn't you rather have a small, tight-knit group bonding around you rather than an expensive army of experts slowing you down? Specialization is the norm today, but review the people you're considering to work with on your dream-team. How deep do they run? I'll bet all of them have several—even many—talents besides what's on their business cards.

Friendly Competition
"There's no time for fussing and fighting, my friend…"
("We Can Work It Out," 1965)

When you think of *competition*, you may think of it in the athletic sense: two boxers going head-to-head, two pro football teams battling it out, winner take all. However, in the Beatles way, competition is a friendly sport, even an affectionate one. The Fabs would compete amongst themselves and with their peers, not to win but rather to better themselves artistically.

This ability to see others as resources and not foes took the Beatles to lofty heights. Here's Paul on the subject: "We'd be on the tour bus, and Roy Orbison was on the back of the bus, and he played us 'Pretty Woman,' and we'd think, 'We've gotta write one as good as that!' We were trying to improve all the time."

George Martin remembered the competition between John and Paul as writers. "Their collaboration as songwriters was never Rodgers and Hart. It was always more Gilbert and Sullivan." He explained the analogy: "If John did something, Paul would wish he'd thought of it, and go away and try to do something better, and vice versa. It was a very healthy spirit of competition." "Yeah," agreed Paul. "This was one of the best things about Lennon and McCartney, the competitive element within the team. It was great!"

Paul recounted a typical friendly studio battle between the Beatles' two guitarists. "George Martin would be saying, 'Can you turn the guitar amps down please?' And John would look at George [Harrison] and say, 'How much are you going down? Let's go down to five, alright?' John would go to six, 'OK, I'm at five!' 'You bugger! You're not! You're at six!' There was always this rivalry."

This friendly rivalry extended to the group's artistic peers. Paul has often cited Beach Boys' leader Brian Wilson as a huge influence on his bass playing and on the group's harmony structures, as far back as "Paperback Writer." He credits Brian's masterpiece, *Pet Sounds*, in 1966 as *the* major inspiration for the Beatles' *Sgt. Pepper* album. Paul said, "When I heard *Pet Sounds*, I thought, 'Oh dear, what the hell are we gonna do?'" He added, "If records had a director within a band, I sort of directed *Pepper*. And my influence was basically the *Pet Sounds* album. John was influenced by it, perhaps not as much as me. It was certainly a record that we all played. It was the record of the time."

This respectful rivalry was mutual. In a 1995 documentary, Brian Wilson noted, "We prayed for an album that would be a rival to *Rubber Soul* [released at the end of 1965]. He added, "It was a prayer, but there was some ego there . . . but it worked. *Pet Sounds* happened immediately."

The Beach Boys–Beatles rivalry continued. With the impending release of *Sgt. Pepper*, Paul visited the Beach Boys' Los Angeles studio, where they were painstakingly recording their follow-up to *Pet Sounds*. Before leaving, Paul played and sang "She's Leaving Home," good-naturedly warning Brian Wilson as he left, "You'd better hurry up!" Sadly, Brian lost his way due to his drug dependency, and the album *Smile* was never completed.

John's American artistic rival and counterpart was Bob Dylan, whose influence began seeping into the Beatles' music as early as "I'll Cry Instead" from *A Hard Day's Night* and through *Help!* and *Rubber Soul*. Like-wise, Dylan, knowing that the Beatles' sound was the future of music, switched from his solo folk act in late 1965 to a full rock-band format.

Relatedly, Paul discussed one his most aggressive rockers, "Helter Skelter": "Pete Townsend said to the press that his group [the Who] had just recorded a song that was the loudest, the most raucous rock 'n' roll, the dirtiest thing they'd ever done. Well, that made me think, 'Right! We've got to do that!' And we decided to do the loudest, nastiest, sweati-est rock number we could."

John Sebastian, leader of the Lovin' Spoonful, a hit U.S. group at the time, said this of *Sgt. Pepper*: "It was like the Beatles had thrown down a hat in the center of a ring, it was a tremendous challenge. I remember hav-ing just finished an album that was fairly complex in its arrangement and then hearing this incredible pile of tracks, with stuff going backwards, entire orchestras playing unconventionally, and mechanical tricks we'd never heard before. It seemed like an almost insurmountable task to come up with anything even in the same ballpark."

The Fabs were quite generous with their creative output. One example of their generosity enabled the Rolling Stones to have their first huge break, just when they needed one. The Stones had achieved a bit of notoriety with their first record (a cover of Chuck Berry's "Come On"), but there was some concern from the record company about a follow-up, as the group was not yet writing its own material. John and Paul paid the group a quick visit on the way to a concert and finished off a tune the Beatles were working on, "I Wanna Be Your Man," in less than twenty minutes, tailoring it specifically for the Stones. This one gave the Stones their first top-ten record.

John relayed the story: "'I Wanna Be Your Man' was a kind of lick Paul had, and Mick and Keith had heard we had an unfinished song. We played a rough version to them and they said, 'Yeah, OK, that's our style.' But it was only really a lick, so Paul and I went off in the corner of the room and finished the song off while they were all sitting there talking. We came back, and that's how Mick and Keith got inspired to write—because they said, 'Jesus, look at that! They just went in the corner and wrote it!'"

Paul said of this continuing relationship with the Stones, "I think George [Harrison] had been instrumental in getting them their first major record contract. We suggested them to Decca Records because that company had blown it by refusing us, so they had tried to save face by asking George, 'Know any other groups?' He said, 'Well, there is this group called the Rolling Stones.' So that's how they got their contract."

This friendly relationship with the Rolling Stones didn't prevent the Beatles from defending their turf. Responding in 1971 to disparaging comments the Stones were making of the Beatles, John noted, "I would like to just list what we did and what the Stones did. Everything we did, Mick [Jagger] did exactly the same. He imitated us. You know *Satanic Majesties* is *Sgt. Pepper* and [the Stones'] 'We Love You' is [the Beatles'] 'All You Need Is Love.' I resent the implication that the Rolling Stones are like revolutionaries and that the Beatles weren't. The Stones are not in the same class, music-wise or power-wise, never were."

What's your view on competition? Is it all about winning, winning, winning? The Beatles way means competing on a friendly basis! Unheard of! But try competing with your peers on a higher level—one of mutual respect and admiration. It makes so much sense. Being protective, or worse, jealous, will ultimately make you petty, guarded, and small. Acknowledging, appreciating, and learning from your peers will surely help your dreams reach untold heights.

YOU'RE THE FIFTH BEATLE! — *Team*

Here are several exercises for being fab that center on leadership, team-work, and deploying a healthy competitiveness:

★ Who's the leader? If you decide it's you, are you willing to take on the responsibilities of managing that team, of constantly being *up*, of taking charge during the good times and bad? Remember what Ringo said about John: "He was like our own little Elvis. Very forceful, very funny, very bright, and always someone for us to look up to." Will your team members have similar accolades to say about you? Paul's leadership qualities, which came to the fore later in the Fab's career, were similar to John's. What traits do you have that will produce great results from your own team? For John and Paul, their own willingness to work long and hard at their craft moti-vated the others. Over the next several days, mirror these traits of hard work, tenacity, dedication, and loyalty. These traits are a few of what's required to follow the Beatles way. Make them your way!

★ What kind of hard choices are you willing to make? Do you think you could go as far as firing someone who worked with you in the trenches for two years, as the group felt necessary to do with Pete Best? Could you put your ego aside in the sacrificial act of allowing equally talented people into your dream, as John did in letting Paul and George into his group, the Quarrymen?

★ While the core four Beatles were the central force behind their dream, they created a magnificent inner circle of people they trusted and engaged—not merely hired. Whom do you know who you could engage this way? How would you do it? Are your dream and your persona compelling enough to ensure the kind of loyalty you'll need to inspire people to work hard at thankless—but much needed—tasks for the group?

★ Being fab means competing with yourself and your immediate team, such as Paul and John did on their songwriting, but also with peers you respect. Whom do you respect enough to compete with, or are you merely trying to beat out a person who is "hot" at the moment? Go out and buy *Pet Sounds* by the Beach Boys, and give it a thorough listen. Could your dream inspire your peers as much as Brian Wilson's affected the Beatles?

★ How often do you share the benefits you've attained as you see your dreams become realities? Do you generously give of your time and talent to the competition around you? The Beatles did. They were never concerned of "using up" their talent. Rather, they drew on a wellspring of ability and confidence. Can you see the benefits of giving of your abundance and your talents as the Beatles did so often? Can you see how *not* holding on to this abundance or hiding it could make your dream grow ever bigger, ever richer?

5 CONTROL

We had a rule
that came in very early out of sheer practicality,
which was—if we couldn't remember the song the next day, then it was no good.
We assumed if we, who had written it, couldn't remember it,
what chance would an ordinary member of the public have of remembering it?
And it was a rule we stuck to.

—Paul McCartney

Now let's spend some time on a topic of prime importance in the Beatles way: *control*.

Make no mistake, the Beatles created and controlled virtually every aspect of their career from their visual image—clothes, haircuts, stage presence—to the direction and quality of their music and films and to the people involved in making it all happen.

As the epigraph for this chapter shows, their songwriting direction was controlled in-house, never by outsiders. This is important to cite here because, to this day, there's a misperception that the Beatles were led around like naïve simpletons by their manager, their record producer, their record companies, their film producers, and even their wives and girlfriends.

Far from it! This chapter will focus on how the Fabs pretty much charted every course of their career. If they did have help, they enlisted it from someone they had personally scrutinized carefully to ensure that this person would further their dream.

Richard Lester—as director on *A Hard Day's Night* and *Help!*—saw first-hand the Fabs' ability to run their own show: "Right from the beginning,

I'm not sure how many decisions Brian Epstein ever made." He added, "John was a very strong personality, and the boys themselves as a four-headed group of people did *very much* have a say as to what they wanted to do. It would have been very hard to shove an idea down those four throats."

Being Yourself
"Act Naturally"
(*Help!*, 1965)

Let's dig deeper into the "do it yourself" attitude the group brandished throughout their career. Though seemingly ridiculously simple, today this commitment to *naturalness*, to simply "being yourself," is virtually a lost art. We're living in an age of "political correctness" where the wrong comment can raise eyebrows, or worse, damage a career. Everyone—from sports figures to politicians to movie stars—is coached by media experts to say just the right thing. But fab wisdom says be real, be true to your nature, be natural. What a relief!

This may seem obvious, as we all know and love the Beatles for who they were, but think about it. Defying studio desires to craft their image for them, the Beatles smoked cigarettes, drank Scotch mixed with Coca-Cola in public, had outrageously long hair, addressed the mainstream press freely with wisecracks, and later told the world they were proud to have experimented with pills, pot, and LSD. Today, in an era of political correctness, image training, and corporate marketing experts, successful people would be quite unlikely to do this.

"We brought with our records an overall image," noted Paul on the subject of being natural. "We were the first ones in rock 'n' roll that didn't kid the kids about drinking milk, and America was shocked. 'A Scotch and Coke?' they'd ask, 'On TV and radio?' And we'd go, 'Yeah, a Scotch and

Coke?' Or smoking: 'You can't smoke!' We came along and I think we were just honest lads, and it got us into trouble sometimes, but we didn't give in to the hypocrisy. We commented on the world as we saw it. We were honest and our approach was honest. We were straight, and said what we thought, and that shocked a lot of Americans."

This natural, "be yourself" approach worked for the Fabs right out of the box. By 1960, almost half the teenage male population in Liverpool were in rock 'n' roll groups. But most of these groups were copying the U.K. hit act at the time, Cliff Richard and the Shadows, a tamed-down version of Elvis with light pop songs. Not so the Beatles, who stuck to their love of R&B, rock 'n' roll, and soul. This ability to follow what was in their hearts, rather than what was on the charts, made them unique in Liverpool initially—and shortly thereafter in the world at large.

To this point, one of the last albums on the Beatles' Apple record label was John and Yoko's *Two Virgins*, released while the Beatles were still together, which featured the couple stark-naked, baring it all for the world to see. As John said at the time, "We were in love and being relaxed with each other's bodies." Talk about being natural!

One other point that may be filed under the "obvious *un*-obvious" file for being fab is the group's decision *not* to go for impact by shocking the world. They avoided overt sexuality in their performances, either live, on film, or in their recordings. They relied instead on their inherent elegance—you can call it *class*—and of course on their talent and character. And it didn't hurt that they also had the finest tailors and hairstylists in Britain! But selling sex was too easy. It was not what the group was about, *ever*. The Beatles wrote and performed great music with the main lyrical subject being a simple one: love.

Here are a few exchanges from the 1964 Australian tour between John and Paul and the press about being yourself:

Question: "Are you very conscious of your responsibilities? I mean, teenagers dwell on your every comment and action. Do you feel very responsible towards this?"

John: "No, we just sort of behave as normally as we can, you know. We don't feel as though we should preach this and tell 'em that. You know, let 'em do what they like."

Paul: "We never used to believe it when we used to open a magazine, and it'd say, 'So-and-so doesn't drink, doesn't smoke, doesn't go out late.' So we just act normally."

Question: "I know you say you act normally, but how can you, when everywhere you go people go crazy?"

John: "Normal in the environment that surrounds *us.*"

And here's George on the subject in 1964:

Question: "One thing I've noticed about the Beatles is that you don't come on with 'big star' attitudes."

George: "I think that's one of the big points that has contributed to our success, because we've always been naturals. We've always disliked that sort of phony star-image, you know, we'd much rather be ourselves. We've always thought, 'If they don't like us how we are, then "hard luck."' And they did like us, you know. People like natural people better I think."

Later, George reflected deeper: "There was an honesty we had, a very simple, naïve honesty, and I think that had a lot to do with where we came from as well. Everybody who comes out of Liverpool thinks they're a comedian, and we were no exception. And it was that which kept us going, that got us through a lot of bad times."

Next to being natural, being fab also meant fighting back when necessary. As is their job, the mainstream press worked relentlessly to provoke the group into a controversial comment or into making some sort of faux pas that could run on the front page. But being natural does not mean you have to let others take you for a fool. Those who went over the line were quickly met with a sharp reproach from all four, as you can clearly see by these comments at an early press conference:

John: "We've been quoted as being rude to people. We're always rude back, you know."

Paul: "If someone comes up to us and is rude to us, then we'd be idiots to sort of stand there and smile as they were being rude to us, you know. I mean, nobody is gonna take that. And it doesn't matter if they're a public figure or anything. You know, you're just stupid if you don't do something in return. It's OK turning the other cheek, you know. But (*laughs*) your cheek often get smashed up that way!"

John, in particular, would walk out of a function if he felt the group was being treated poorly, and Paul would often sign a fake name for pushy autograph seekers. They were no slaves to their quest for stardom. No goal, in the Beatles way, is worth sacrificing your self-respect.

How natural is your lifestyle? Do you feel completely comfortable in word and deed as you go through your day? When someone's rude to you, do you dare speak your mind openly, or do you stare at your shoes and take it? When you're in a meeting at work, do you speak your mind freely, or do you find safety in silence? Being fab is being natural—not acting toward what you perceive others might want from you, or worse, trying to be what others dictate to you. This one principle can completely alter your lifestyle forever if you act on it. Give it a try: The next time somebody cuts in front of you at the supermarket, swallow your fear and speak up! "Excuse me," you'll say. "You can come first, after me!"

The Naming Convention

"You, you know, you know my name..."

("You Know My Name," the flip side of the single "Let It Be," 1969)

As we've already seen, the Beatles took seriously Mahatma Gandhi's advice to "create and preserve the image of your choice." The Beatles lived this philosophy both in their overarching dream of success and in the small but important everyday details.

For starters, the Fabs kept their own birth names. This was at a time when most in the Liverpool rock scene were changing theirs to such flashy names as Billy Fury, Rory Storm, and Tommy Steele. Except for Ringo Starr, who had changed his name from Richard Starkey before joining the group, names like John Lennon, Paul McCartney, and George Harrison were not exactly "show-biz" zingers. Again, they believed that talent alone would be reason enough to make them famous and respected.

And of course, there's the simple genius of the group name, "the Beatles." No record company promotional-type sat around dreaming up some clever moniker for the Fabs. It was devised by them directly out of their musical heritage. While it's not clear who came up with the name—some accounts say Stu Sutcliffe, and some say John—it definitely comes from the Fabs' love of Texas rocker Buddy Holly, whose backup band was "the Crickets."

With their Liverpudlian love of wordplay, they changed "Beetle" to "Beatle," a name that to this day people find appealing for its elegant wit. Brian Epstein wrote in his book, *A Cellarful of Noise*, "I wonder what would have happened if the group had been named 'The Liverpool Lads'?" Indeed.

The habit of coming up with compelling names didn't end there. The Fabs named their first movie *A Hard Day's Night* courtesy of Ringo. According to Beatle lore, after a long day of filming, Ringo was leaving the studio, saying, "It's been a hard day," and walking outside into the night, adding "'s night." It also appears in the pages of John's first book, *In His Own Write*, published at the time the movie was being filmed. In it, the short story "Sad Michael" features the line, "He'd had a hard day's night that day, for Michael was a Cocky Watchtower."

For the film *Help!*, the group was not intimidated into accepting the title *Eight Arms to Hold You* devised by the screenwriter, even when Capitol in the United States prematurely printed it on the first singles and advertisements preceding the film. Rather, it's likely that one of the group came up with it. If you listen closely to the scene where Ringo is being kidnapped by "mad scientists," you'll hear him shouting, "*Help! Help me!*" It's not hard to imagine John thinking, "Hmm ... now *that's* a good title!" "We had a couple of ideas, but they just didn't click," said Paul of this process. "It's got to be a title that all four of us will click our fingers at and say, 'This is it!' Like *A Hard Day's Night*, we knew straight away that was the title we wanted."

Another evidence of their control over their business was in the naming of their company Apple Corps Ltd. Besides being a lovely pun, the name was based on something in their own lives. The name and the green apple logo sprang from Paul's admiration of a René Magritte painting he owned entitled "Le Jeu de Mourre" (The guessing game). Paul explained, "We were sitting around wondering, 'What shall we call this thing?' A is for Apple. That should be the name of the company? Then I thought, 'Wow that Magritte apple is very much "an apple," a big green apple.' I told the ad man about it."

The name became lucrative in a totally unforeseen way a decade after the company's inception. Paul said, "One of the most successful things we did was copyright [trademark] the name. We suspected that someone would nick it and put stuff out. Years later, when Apple Computers started, we went to them and said, 'Excuse us, we've got the name Apple.

You can't trade under that name.' They said, 'We're very big now, we're going to be giants in the computer world.' We said, 'Well, we'll do a deal then,' and we did a deal for a quite a large amount of money."

Controlling your own naming concepts might seem important only if you're expecting a baby. Not true! Whether you're starting your own business or writing a screenplay, the name is of huge concern. For example, Intel spent hundreds of thousands of dollars to come up with a new product name after it had successfully marketed its 286, 386, and 486 personal-computer microprocessors. Logically, the company could have chosen 586, but it desired something fresh. From the Greek root *penta* for "five," the Pentium chip is now a household word, so much so that many computers are inaccurately dubbed "Pentium computers."

Creating Your Image

"And the way she looked was way beyond compare..."
("I Saw Her Standing There," 1963)

Their look, too, was mission-critical to the Fabs. They worked on it from the get-go and refined it throughout their career. Consider the Beatlemania look: controlled, slightly sexual, even somewhat androgynous. In photos, they devised and stayed with this defining look: the neck of Paul's distinctive Hofner bass guitar was always pointing left; staid-yet-smiling George stood in the middle; and John appeared on the right, his black-and-white Rickenbacker reflecting the spotlights, its neck pointing right. And of course there's Ringo in back, on a three-foot pedestal, perched on his stool like some presiding wise man, with the group's elegantly printed name in large type on the front of his kick drum.

No detail is too small when you're going for your dreams the Beatles way. There's the head-and-hair shake the Beatles perfected on their "woo!" on the early hits. This was deliberately devised, despite being mocked by their early Liverpool musical peers. And of course, there's the Beatle bow—that deep, appreciate-your-applause bow that so endeared millions to the group. Paul said of that ingenious move, "We actually used to count the bow: one, two, three—as we'd do this big uniform bow all at once."

And don't think it was Brian Epstein who pushed the group to ditch their early preference for wearing matching leather outfits. Paul sets us straight: "The leather gear was old-hat anyway, and we had already decided we looked ridiculous dressed in all-leather. We got the impression some people were laughing at us, and we looked like a gang of idiots. Brian Epstein suggested we wear ordinary suits—he believed that would be very good for us. I would tend to agree with his stagy ideas. I don't think any of us had any problem with that, or we wouldn't have done it."

Let's move on to the haircuts. *Those* haircuts. When originally sported by their hip Hamburg artist friends like Astrid Kirchherr and Jurgen Vollmer, the cut was much shorter. John and Paul decided to leave their hair longer in the back, so it was a combination of the Hamburg cut and their own fashion ideas.

On John's twenty-first birthday, he received one hundred pounds from a relative, so he and Paul decided to take a holiday to Spain. "We hitch-hiked out of Liverpool," remembered Paul, "got as far as Paris, and decided to stop there for a week. And eventually we got our haircut by Jurgen Vollmer, and that ended up being the 'Beatle haircut.'"

During this same visit, Jurgen took John and Paul to a Parisian flea market, where they bought short "mod-style" jackets. They'd been searching for jackets like that since they fell in love with a collarless jacket worn by their friend Stu Sutcliffe in their Hamburg days. These coats later became the standard early Beatlemania-era jacket. The Beatle boots worn during those days were again born of their own choice, influenced from those early Hamburg days.

The Beatles' attention to image gave them a huge edge in other areas. For instance, they also designed their own album covers to be artistic statements, so much so that these covers are still emulated. This attention to cover design began with their second album as they worked with their chosen photographer, Robert Freeman, who'd been photographing them on tour and whom they also liked personally. For the famed cover of *With the Beatles*, George said that the group brought photographs that Astrid Kirchherr had taken of them in Hamburg—which featured their faces half-in-shadow and unsmiling—and asked Freeman, "Why can't you do it like *this*?"

Paul was integrally involved in concepts for album covers. He brought preliminary sketches to Peter Blake, the artist the group had chosen to help create the *Sgt. Pepper* cover. In another instance, Paul took a commanding interest in the sleeve for the *White Album*. And as a fan of avant-garde artist Richard Hamilton, Paul sought his advice for the *White Album*. Hamilton suggested that after the wildly colorful *Pepper* cover, it might behoove the group to make the new cover simple, using an elegant white background along with an "artsy, limited edition" style of having each record numbered. Additionally, the name "The Beatles" would be slightly raised, in embossed letters. Paul loved and approved those ideas. He also worked personally with Hamilton, arranging the photos for the poster enclosed with the album. Paul's attention to detail is also evident on *Abbey Road*. He brought his sketches to its cover photo-shoot, the famous shot of the group crossing a road. Paul's early conceptualization of the scene is complete with the famed crossing stripes.

Whew! Indeed, the Beatles took a concerted interest in their image from their modest beginnings as Elvis-style greasers, to leather-clad roughnecks, to pop-star princes, to flower children, to stylish hippies. They knew the importance of keeping their look unique, ahead of its time, and always compelling. This image-control principle cannot be underestimated, for while the Beatles' music is the group's artistic legacy, imagine the group if they'd just been four "Joe Schmoes" in ragged T-shirts at any point in their colorful career.

How does this principle affect you on a daily basis? Do you dress up only on special occasions, or do you really work at your look and think about its impact on the likelihood of achieving your goal? Does your image reflect who you are inside? For the Beatles, their naturalness included being fashion-conscious. They enjoyed dressing sharply and being clean-cut and elegant during their early days. Later, their look blossomed into the ultra flower-power *Sgt. Pepper* regalia. Even later the four maturing Beatles went for the more comfortable hippie-style still emulated today by fashion designers who specialize in the "I don't care" look.

Fashion looks may seem superficial, but the point is that they are under your control. Before people know you, they'll be judging you on your appearance. What first impression do you want them to have? What kind of clothes and name do you need to make that impression?

Working Environment
"When I'm home, everything seems to be right..."
("A Hard Day's Night," 1964)

Let's not forget the obvious here, however. Despite the unique image (long haircuts, suits, boots), for the Beatles the most significant and lasting component of being fab was producing a quality product.

When it came to the music, the Beatles adhered to a self-imposed stratospheric standard of excellence and elegance. There was no letup in the group's total and unequivocal control over every aspect of their music, from the songwriting to the performances—and to the recording techniques.

So let's take a close look at just who ran the studio during those Beatle recording sessions. Do you think it was producer George Martin? Well, certainly he did so in the very early goings, but here's this telling comment from Paul: "When *Sgt. Pepper* came out, the reviews said it was 'George Martin's finest album' and we went, 'What? *What?*' I mean George Martin was great! He's a lovely guy, and we all loved him. But don't get the idea for one minute that he did it. He was the producer, fine, but he couldn't have made this album with say Gerry and the Pacemakers!"

John said of the Beatles' time with George Martin, "We did a lot of learning together." And George Martin himself has said, "Paul and John were the prime movers of *Sgt. Pepper*—their inspiration, their creation of the original ideas, was absolutely paramount. I was merely serving them in trying to get those ideas down." Paul reiterated the point: "One thing people don't generally know was that John or I, or whoever was involved in the orchestral side, would go round to George Martin's house or he would come round to ours, and we would sit with him [and go over the arrangements]."

George Martin has never denied the Beatles' skillfulness and inventiveness in the studio, especially after the group quickly learned the ins and outs of the work required: "At the start, I was like a master with his pupils; they knew nothing about recording. But by the end, I was to be the servant while they were the masters."

In addition, the group also had to literally design their own creative aura inside the hospital-like environs of the EMI-owned Abbey Road studios, even during the halcyon days of Beatlemania. In fact, while the group's touring tenacity was critical to the Beatles' success, their dedication to the work inside the recording studio reveals an astounding durability as well, under less-than-perfect circumstances. George Harrison remarked recently, "It was all very clinical at Abbey Road, so we had to create the atmosphere." He added, "After a number of years, we finally asked them if we could have some colored lights, or a dimmer brought in [to break up the monotony of the harsh fluorescent overhead lighting system]. After asking them for three years, they finally brought in this big steel stand with a couple of red and blue neon lamps on it."

George added that even the studio cafeteria's refrigerator had a padlock on it, so if the group wanted a cup of tea after hours, they'd have to literally break open the padlock on the fridge just to get to a spot of milk. "We had to do that every night for five years! It wasn't like they realized, 'Oh, they drink tea after six o'clock, so we'll leave the fridge open.' No, they padlocked it each time!"

The bread and butter of the Beatles was their music. And they cared for and nurtured every detail of the environment where they created that music—right down to the lighting and tiny "fridge" in their beloved studio.

How does this attention to detail apply to you? Well, say you've been thinking of starting a home business where you'll be working from eight to ten hours a day. Have you created an environment that's comfortable and relaxed, a place where your creativity will be nurtured? Perhaps you've got your own ongoing business or an office that you just *cannot* get any work done in. Take a look around. What about remodeling the space to suit your inner persona? How about the rest of your home? Have you created a cozy and welcoming family room—a spot where the family meets to nurture each other—with good books and good music?

Attention to Detail
"Every Little Thing"
(*Beatles for Sale*, 1964)

Control means not only a rigid adherence to your original dream but the ability to adapt to outside influences and to use them as tools to better yourself.

The Beatles, throughout their career, kept close watch on the charts and their musical peers. The willingness to participate in friendly competition while at the same time learning from your peers is a factor in living life the Beatles way. Paul, for example, has said that the Lovin' Spoonful's "Daydream" was responsible for the feel of his cheery song "Good Day Sunshine." He also credits Canned Heat's unplugged style of the late '60s as an influence on his song "Two of Us" and for the overall concept behind the return-to-roots music of *Let It Be*.

Oh yes, they were listening to—and studying—the records of their time. In an interview during the Beatlemania days, a reporter tried to bait Paul with a query on the new number-one song on the British charts by the Animals. The reporter wanted to know whether or not the Animals' hit, "House of the Rising Sun," meant an end to the reign of Beatle hits. But Paul answered immediately, "Of course not." And having already studied the record in detail, he noted that Bob Dylan had actually arranged and recorded the song years earlier.

Besides the Dylan influence on many of John's mid-period Beatle songs, the Beach Boys' vocal arrangements and records obviously affected "Paperback Writer" and the freshness of "Penny Lane." Paul has said he wanted a "Beach Boys-y cleanness" on that song. And the Beach Boys were influential on the surf-style "Back in the U.S.S.R." In fact, Mike Love, lead singer of the Beach Boys, suggested the lyrical theme of the "Ukraine and Moscow girls" à la "California Girls" during a conversation with Paul at Maharishi Mahesh Yogi's retreat in India.

And the song "Hello Goodbye," written by Paul during a limbo period at the end of 1967, was actually a smart move. That record was the Beatles' timely answer to the prevailing bubblegum sound popularized at the time by groups such as the Monkees and Tommy James and the Shondells.

Keeping a close eye on the smallest of details that make up a dream was an essential part of being fab for the Beatles. Not only did they keep their eyes on the music charts and their ears on music released by their peers, but they literally made every second of their records count.

To cite just one example of many, take "I Want to Hold Your Hand." The introduction alone is compelling, as it *doesn't* initially offer up the "home" key of the song, instead deploying the "trick" of beginning the song with the last bars of the song's middle section (the "I can't hide" section). This is enhanced by a forced beat, which leaves the listener unsure of what the actual rhythm is going to be, and this is compounded by having the vocals enter two beats ahead of the verse proper ("Oh yeah, I . . ."). There's also the musical arrangement of the middle section, which glimmers with arpeggios (playing of the tones of a chord in rapid succession rather than simultaneously). On top of that, there's also those joyful handclaps, which give a personal touch to the record. And to complete this mini-symphony of dazzling effects, the group brings their performance to a breathless close on two syncopated bars in 3/8 time. All this in just under two minutes and twenty-four seconds!

If you listen closely to "If I Fell" from the movie *A Hard Day's Night*, you'll notice that Paul's voice noticeably cracks on the word "vain" in the line "And I would be sad if our new love was in *vain*!" And in "Day Tripper," there's just one note missing from that catchy guitar riff toward the end of the record. These seeming mistakes were added intentionally. John has said the group made an effort to add something "off" in several of their songs to "see if anybody'd notice."

And here's a little-known story regarding the animal noises in "Good Morning, Good Morning" from *Sgt. Pepper*. The apparently random farmyard noises during the fade were actually designed, on John's insistence, as a sequence in which each successive animal is capable of eating its predecessor! Talk about attention to detail!

Fab wisdom says that attention to detail includes such minutiae as consciously dropping one guitar note from a hit song! Consider your focus on the small items that make up your dream plans. Are you up on the latest trends your goals are targeted toward? How many related magazines and newspapers do you subscribe to in your prospective field? Do you take the time to review the ins and outs of the projects you're developing? On the home front, are you involved with your children on a day-to-day basis? Maybe it's time to roll up your sleeves and dig deeply into the details of your own life and the integral people involved.

Caring for Your Audience
"Thank You Girl"
(The flip side of the single "Please Please Me," 1963)

As well as maintaining a consistently high quality in their recordings, the subject matter of the Beatles' songs, specifically in the early days, was geared directly toward their audience. In fact, you could call these fans their "customers," though the love the group had for their fans went deeper than that. This early decision to write songs directly to their fans was actually born of a deep emotional love for them. The Beatles could relate to their fans because they had known a similar love for their own idols, such as Elvis, Little Richard, and Chuck Berry.

And this love affair began right away, at the group's early signs of success. "We probably loved the Cavern audiences best of anything. It was fantastic," said George of that time in the very early '60s. "We never lost our identification with the audience all the time. We were not like the other groups who kept on copying [the Shadows, a hit group of the time]. We were playing to our own fans, who were like us. We enjoyed it, and so did they."

George was even more direct on this point in 1964: "Whatever way you look at it, the Beatles, and every other group in the top twenty, rely entirely on the fans. It would be no good finding a good song and making a terrific recording of it if there were no fans around to decide whether they liked it or not." He added, "To any artist, fans are vitally important.

An artist who did well and then wanted to forget about his fans might as well forget about his fame at the same time."

Paul explained this admiration for fans in retrospect: "We knew that if we wrote a song called 'Thank You Girl,' that a lot of the girls who wrote us fan letters would take it as a genuine 'thank you.' So a lot of our early songs were directly addressed to the fans." And here's John in an unguarded moment commenting on the group's concern for their fans. Once when his driver tried to stop fans from overwhelming his Rolls-Royce, John instructed, "Leave them alone! They bought it, and they've got the right to smash it up!"

Relatedly, at a Beatles press conference in Sydney, Australia, in June 1964, the group discussed why they stood in a near-typhoon simply to wave to their fans at an airport reception:

George: "Seeing as the fans got soaked though, well, we didn't mind, did we?"
Reporter: "The kids have been waiting all night, and they appreciated it."
John: "Well, they deserved it, didn't they, waiting all night."

Further, the Beatles kept their official fan club going, despite the fact it never turned a profit. Besides sending out over forty thousand bulletins and posters several times a year, there were the salaries and office rentals and expenses for two full-time officials coordinating forty voluntary staff at forty worldwide branches.

There was also a spoken-word Christmas message recorded annually by the group and distributed to fan-club members on flexi-disc. And the last year the group was together (1970), though they couldn't find time to record a Christmas message—by then they had pretty much broken up—they instead issued a full album's worth of all seven years of the Beatles holiday fan-club recordings.

This willingness to please their fans prevailed even after Beatlemania had quieted down and as the group began planning the *Sgt. Pepper* album.

Paul said of that project, "Our idea was to give people a damn fine record, one where you get a thick cover which lasts and lasts for years. You'd get goodies, freebies [such as free badges and buttons, lyrics printed for the first time, and a gatefold cover], all for the price of a regular record." He noted, "The record company kept saying, 'No, that'll increase the price!' We fought like devils I tell you. But I see no reason why you shouldn't fight for things like that. All we're trying to do is give people a great deal, and they'll buy more in the end, because it's a great deal, they'll come back for the next one, so it seemed very wise to us."

Paul explained further the fab mind-set for pleasing their fans during the design for *Pepper*. "[When I was a kid], I would go in on a Saturday morning, to a place in Liverpool called Lewis' with my ten bob, buy my record, and then sit on the bus for a half-an-hour afterwards, and read the cover. I'd take it out of the bag, read it, read the label, read anything I could get my eyes on. So on *Pepper*, I thought, 'This is it, it's an overall concept,' we'll have the cover packed with little things, so three months from now you'll go, 'Oh I never saw that!' The whole idea was to put everything, the whole world into this package."

Ringo summed up the "being fab" attitude for their fans back in 1964 with this sincere quote: "It's the fans who make you, without them, you're nothing. We love the fans as much as they love us."

Your dream most likely includes people, right? You need to please other people—your children, your customers, your co-workers—to make your dream a reality. Right? OK, how deeply do you consider what these people want and need from you? The Beatles *loved* their audience and proved it with extracurricular work tailored just for them. The Beatles way, for you, asks the same.

Let's say you're a painter—an artist. How often do you think about the reaction from the people who view your work, or the potential "customers." Who'd be willing to actually *pay* for it? The Beatles truly *catered* to their audience. If you don't appreciate the word *catered*, then you need to reconsider. The Beatles catered to their audience year in and year out from their beginnings at the Cavern right up until the end of their career.

Being Different at Any Cost

"If there's anything that you want, if there's anything I can do..."

("From Me to You," 1963)

Though thwarted at every turn by the U.S. arm of their record company (Capitol Records), the Fabs kept their attention to detail on the British releases of their records, in which they could maintain some form of control.

In fact, when Capitol Records virtually created a new Beatles album by assembling various leftover tracks and releasing them as a "new" product entitled *'Yesterday'...and Today* on June 15, 1966, the phenomenon was nothing new. In the eighteen-month period between January 1964 and June 1966, Capitol—and the United Artists record label—managed to release nearly twice as many Beatles albums in America as had been issued by Britain's EMI Parlophone, the Beatles' home label.

Capitol and UA had accomplished that feat through a variety of means: issuing fewer songs per album (typically eleven, as opposed to fourteen on the Beatles' U.K. records); adding tracks released as singles (typically not included on U.K. albums); and padding film soundtracks with instrumentals from the Beatle films. Understandably, with their desire to give their fans—their customers—100 percent, the Beatles hated it.

Here's the group discussing this topic after the release of the *Help!* album in 1965. For the American version, Capitol had included only seven original Beatle songs and padded the rest with George Martin's incidental film music.

Question: "I understand that the record album *Help!* has different numbers in the English version than in the United States version. Is this true, and if so, why?"

Paul: "The thing is, Capitol issues all sort of mad stuff, you know. It's nothing to do with us. We take fourteen tracks to be put out, but they keep a couple and put them out later. But it's a drag, because we make an album to be like an album, to be a complete thing."

John: "We plan it, and they wreck it."

Paul: "No offense, Capitol, but we send it over here and you put the movie score soundtrack on it. And, you know, if someone is gonna buy one of our records, I think they want to hear us, and not sound-track music."

George: "They even change the photographs off the front and put something daft on."

But the fans in the United Kingdom—whom the Fabs used as their personal barometer during their ongoing success—were given only the newest numbers the group produced and were never charged twice for the same song. John explained why this kind of scheming conducted by Capitol and UA was anathema to the group: "In the early days, we were really set on giving people their money's worth off a record," he said. "And that was our policy, to put fourteen tracks aside that were brand new, we never put singles on the album. That was what everybody else did—was to have a hit single and make an album around it."

Occasionally you might find your dream out of your control, as the Beatles did when their U.S. record company exploited their original creative directions. However, fab wisdom says to keep your focus on what you can control. Giving energy to the negative aspects of your dream's journey will only serve to expand those aspects. Work that much harder on infusing excellence into what you truly want—not what you don't.

Testing It Out

"You're gonna say you love me too..."
("I Should Have Known Better," 1964)

How do you know your dream is succeeding? One sure fab method is to keep your eye on the sales of your product. Obviously that's one factor the Beatles never had reason to be concerned with. To ensure the continuing quality of their work, the group had an in-house "market test" they used as a yardstick. Here's Paul on the subject, during an interview in 1964 with talk-show host David Frost:

Frost: "How do you judge a good song when you've written it?"
Paul: "By us liking it, you know, John and I. If we like it, if we think it's a 'good'un.' It's a combination of liking it, and [knowing and studying] what is commercial, what we think other people will like."
Frost: "Can it be a good song if you like it, and nobody was to buy it? That hasn't happened to you."
Paul: "It always is for us: If we like it. And in fact, we don't like bad songs, that's all there is to it."

This kind of market testing began back in their rock 'n' roll incubators of the Liverpool Cavern club and during their tenure in Hamburg. Trying out an array of new songs before a live audience was an effective means of finding out what worked and what didn't.

Before the screaming audiences became the norm for the Beatles' live performances, which nullified this technique, it worked astoundingly well. In fact, before they hit the U.S. charts—with five records in the top five—they'd already produced a backlog of hits in the United Kingdom for nearly two years. This included four number-one singles, all of which had been tried and tested before live audiences.

The Beatles were also diligent about listening to the work they'd accomplished at every studio session, most of which ran into the early morning hours. This meant having personal copies made of their daily recording efforts for their listening at home. These "rough mixes" can take a good amount of time to produce—sometimes nearly as long as mixing a finished record—while an exhausted group has to wait for the engineers to produce them. However, this homework would prove immensely useful time and again, as the group could gauge by these home listenings what needed improvement and what was usable, enabling the following day's session to be even more productive.

You probably gave up on homework when you graduated from college, but if you're living life the Beatles way, doing homework on your dream is a natural activity. Sure, you spent a large part of your day making your dream a reality, but what do you do in the off-hours at night and on weekends? Are you spending time at the local pub or shopping mall or standing in line at the movie theater in town? The Beatles took home the day's work of their recording sessions and spent long hours into the night figuring out ways to make the next day's sessions even better.

Publicize Yourself

"Dear Sir or Madam, will you read my book . . . ?"
("Paperback Writer," 1966)

A do-it-yourself attitude and attention to detail permeated every aspect of being fab, even when it came to the Beatles promoting themselves. An example from 1960 is found in seventeen-year-old Paul's four-hundred-word letter written to a journalist he met in a pub after a show. "Dear Mr. Lowe," reads the note, "I am sorry about the time I have taken to write to you, but I hope I have not left it too late. Here are some details about the group.... It consists of four boys: Paul McCartney (guitar), John Lennon (guitar), Stuart Sutcliffe (bass) and George Harrison (another guitar)...."

The willingness to self-promote is evident in the energy the group put forth for their U.K.-released 45-rpm records. If you think of these singles as advertisements, then a group who gets on the radio with one of them is, in essence, receiving free advertising. Accordingly, the care on Beatle singles is easy to spot: Nineteen out of twenty-two single releases went to number one in the United Kingdom. In America, the total number-one records was twenty-five out of a possible thirty-two releases. This kind of airplay virtually ensured immense sales and an ongoing interest in the group. George made a humorous observation on why the Beatles had bigger fan receptions than the queen of England: "Well, she never had a hit record, did she?"

At the height of Beatlemania, a related self-marketing tool was deployed in John's two books, *In His Own Write* and *A Spaniard in the Works*. These critically acclaimed works further promoted the Beatles as intelligent and literate, taking them well out of the simplistic image of a "here today, gone tomorrow" pop band and driving the mainstream populace to take the group seriously.

For the Beatles, being fab meant not minding the crowded marketplace of Beatle-posers—all hair, suits, boots, and some of them even able to knock out Beatle-like hits on occasion. Here's an insightful observation early on from John about the matter: "Well, I suppose a couple of people have jumped on the bandwagon, but it doesn't really matter because it promotes the whole idea of us. If we're away on tour, there's still a few 'little Beatles' around to remind people of us."

Self-promotion techniques were used successfully even toward the end of the group's career, notably by John, who in the middle of recording the *Abbey Road* album took time off to work on a series of "Bed-Ins for Peace." John explained at the time, "We're trying to make Christ's message contemporary. What would *he* have done if he had advertisements, records, films, TV and newspapers? Christ made miracles to tell his message. Well, the miracle today is communications, so let's use it." He explained further, "The point of this Bed-In in a nutshell is a *commercial* for peace, as opposed to a commercial for war, which is on the news everyday in the newspapers. Henry Ford knew how to sell cars by advertising. I'm selling peace, and Yoko and I are just one big advertising campaign. Publicity is our game—because of the Beatles, that's the trade I've learned."

Self-promotion might be anathema to you. It might sound selfish, even petty. But listen to John Lennon compare his message of peace with the message of Jesus. John justified his use of the media because he felt that his message was important enough to create advertisements and commercials for it. Perhaps your goal isn't as lofty as world peace, but isn't your message important enough to promote? If you're working at being fab— and if your goals, dreams, and ultimate destination is one of peace, love, and brotherhood—then it's probably a safe bet that your dream is indeed an important one for the world at large.

YOU'RE THE FIFTH BEATLE! — *Control*

Here are a few ideas to empower you to take complete and unequivocal control of your dream-making strategies:

★ The Beatles way means being completely natural. Are you truthful in your words and actions, or are you uncomfortable around people, working too hard to try and be natural? Do you think that people will not accept you and your dream if you need to be yourself in order to accomplish it?

This might be a good time to examine your dream. Does the dream feel real to you? Does it feel natural?

★ The Beatles consistently allowed their self-respect to shine through. How people treat you—and how you react—is a great indicator of your own self-respect meter. The next time someone criticizes or insults you, notice how you react. Do you just take it? Or do you explode in anger? Fab wisdom says that if you're centered in your own self-worth, your reaction will be an even-tempered one.

★ The importance of image is integral to being fab. The Beatles controlled every aspect of their look. How much of your image is under your control? Are others giving you directions or opinions when you should be creating and directing your own image as you see fit? Take stock of where you shop or where you get your hair done in light of the dream you're undertaking. Do the clothes you're wearing accurately reflect where you want to be as your dream manifests? Say that your dream is to be a CEO at a corporation. Wearing cheap suits and shoes wouldn't necessarily reflect the image of a self-assured CEO. This seems obvious, but sometimes in life, our shopping habits can get habitual.

★ The Fabs held their audiences—or customers—in high esteem, even in a loving manner. Do you have this amount of respect and love for your own fans or customers? Do you include them as major components in your own dreams?

★ What kind of market test do you have for *your* dream? Try out your dream in a testing environment in order to strengthen it until it's ready for inspection by a larger audience. An example might be in honing your public-speaking skills. Instead of throwing yourself cold into an event you are to speak at, set up a rehearsal with your close friends and family. Get their opinion on what works and what doesn't. Perhaps you've got ambitions to be a writer. Are you sending out manuscripts without having your peers give you some criticism? Fab wisdom says to try out your work with many people, learn from their reactions, hone your craft, and then you'll discover that your work is suddenly in demand!

6 EVOLVE

EMI had very firm rules which we always had to break . . .
it was just that we felt we knew better.
They'd say, "Well our rule book says . . ."
and we'd say "They're out of date, come on, let's move!"
We always wanted things to be different
because we knew that people, generally, always want to move on,
and if we hadn't pushed them,
the guys would have stuck by their rule books.

—Paul McCartney

You've acted on the first five principles of being fab, and by now you should already be experiencing some success. Remember, as it was for the Beatles, the bigger your dreams, the bigger the success you'll be realizing.

So now what? For the Beatles, it meant simply this: Keep dreaming bigger—and manifesting bigger! In a word: *evolve*.

Make no mistake, in being fab, change is *good*, boredom is *good*. Does this sound like a contradiction? Well, think about it. Do you do what the Fabs did and keep evolving after you've accomplished a goal or achieved a dream? Or do you have a tendency to rest on your laurels, get lethargic, or perhaps celebrate your achievements more than you should? For the Beatles, whenever they realized they were bored, it meant only one thing: They were ready for a new challenge.

Here's Paul on the Fab's attitude during the height of Beatlemania as they tried to present their live audiences with their more complex music to no avail. As the group valiantly worked to get their music heard over a literal wall of screams, ". . . that's when the boredom started creeping in a bit, we'd done it so many times." You know what happened next: The

group turned their energies toward the recording studio. The first achievement from that phase of their evolution was their album *Revolver*, which
many music critics today cite as the best rock album of all time.

Paul was succinct on this methodology for the Beatles way to success:
"We were always pushing ahead: *louder, further, longer, more, different.*"
While Paul was speaking largely of their studio efforts, this mind-set permeated every aspect of their fab methodology in living their dreams, aid-
ing the group in creating new ones and finding the excitement and
knowingness within to achieve them.

There's no question that innovation and risktaking in their music was
the Beatles' hallmark. Yet it's less obvious that the Fabs also broke new
ground with their touring, their movies, their business concepts, and in
their personal lifestyles. This willingness to experiment—even outrageously—kept the group well ahead of their competition, and in many
instances, their trailblazing activities set the stage for entire new industries.

For example, the Beatles' live touring led to the use of arenas and stadiums as standard venues for the rock-concert industry. And with the
group's move to mastering the studio, the music industry moved to a more
album-oriented format, leaving behind the "hit-song and rest-filler" mentality that had prevailed for decades. The Fab's progression in the studio
spurred the electronics industry to invent and market new technologies to
achieve ever more sophisticated sounds. And of course, the Beatles' interest in Eastern spirituality helped inspire the New Age movement, today a
multimillion-dollar industry.

The big difference between the Beatles and other groups was their
willingness to *continue* learning. This ensured their evolution, as they
never rested on past achievements. Once they achieved a high level of
success with a formula, they literally "dumped it" and quickly moved on.
This evolution from lovable moptops to unofficial princes to cultural
radicals is unprecedented even today. It proves that a simple willingness

to take a plunge into the unknown—to fully experience it and then to move on—can be a truly effective success methodology.

Risk. Just the mere *word* can scare people from even attempting the simplest thing out of the ordinary. What about you? What does *risk* mean to you? Do you feel comfortable with Paul's notion that the Beatles should work to be *"louder, further, longer, more, different"*? How much more exciting could your life be by simply incorporating one or two of those words into your daily routine?

Going Underground
"Tell Tchaikovsky the news ..."
("Roll Over Beethoven," 1963)

Immediately after the breakthrough *Rubber Soul* album, which showed the group embracing a more subtle musicianship, Paul and John moved into the underground avant-garde art, performance, film, and music scene in London.

One of their favorite artists was Karlheinz Stockhausen. This Cologne-born classical composer's work preceded today's recording technique of sampling (mixing recorded sound snippets into an original recording). Along the way he created some of the most critically acclaimed avant-garde classical compositions since the mid-'50s, and today he is still creating works that influence classical musicians.

Accordingly, the first Beatles song created for the 1966 album *Revolver* was "Tomorrow Never Knows," John's experimental spiritual-centric epiphany of sound. By then, all four Fabs were recording unique sounds such as barking dogs, train whistles, and the like in their home studios for incorporation into their songs.

Even before John's "Revolution 9" for the 1968 *White Album*, Paul had already created a Stockhausen-influenced recording in late 1966, and he brought the group right along with him. Paul was asked to contribute a song for the "Carnival of Light" event that was being promoted as the London underground's concept of bringing art to the community—in this case, in the form of light shows and experimental music and films.

Under Paul's direction, the Beatles produced an experimental tape that ran fourteen minutes long. It features hypnotic drum and organ sounds, distorted lead guitar, the sound of a church organ, and various effects drenched in tape echo and manic tambourine. Though Paul's work has yet to be released to the public, this avant-garde experimentation by the Fabs later appeared on the pre–*Sgt. Pepper* song "Strawberry Fields Forever" and reached crystallization on the *White Album*. Beatle scholars cite the influence of Stockhausen's 1967 work *Hymnen* on John's "Revolution 9."

Stockhausen is even pictured on the cover of *Sgt. Pepper* amongst the dozens of people the Beatles admired. In 1980, he discussed John's respect for him in a rare press interview: "John often used to phone me. He was particularly fond of my *Hymnen* and *Gesang der Jünglinge* and got many things from them."

Stockhausen's influence was felt especially on the production for "A Day in the Life." "I suggested we write fifteen bars properly so that the orchestra could read it," explained Paul, "but where the fifteen bars began, we would give the musicians a simple direction, 'Start on your lowest note and eventually, at the end of the fifteen bars, be at your highest note.' It all resulted in a crazy crescendo." Paul later said about this famed musical moment, "The orchestra crescendo was based on some of the ideas I'd been getting from Stockhausen, which is abstract—which orchestras are frightened to do. That's not the tradition. But we got 'em to do it!"

Like it, love it, or hate it, this experimental music remains somewhat baffling to the average listener, but it shows an extraordinary artistry—one that makes the Beatles' music compelling and always intriguing. Indeed, Paul still produces "New Age ambient" music to this day, most notably the recording *Rushes* under the "Fireman" pseudonym. We don't have just a group that knocked out repetitious hits year in and year out; we have artists who created music rich in its daringness—and virtually timeless in its longevity.

Again, like it, love it, or hate it, what's your own view on experimentation? Think about how you react when something different comes on the radio or television. Do you switch it off immediately? Or do you give it a chance? By doing so, you're entering into a way of thinking that's pure fab. Try to apply this kind of acceptance of curiosity into your life, your business, and your dreams!

Better yet, you can start right away. Next time you visit your local record store, gravitate away from the "hits" shelf and wander over to the "New Age" section or the classical part of the store. Many record stores allow you to listen before you buy. Try out some CDs by artists you've never heard of. And instead of standing in line for the latest Hollywood blockbuster movie, take in an avant-garde film and analyze your reaction to it. Fab wisdom means trying out new things all the time and incorporating them into your own work and lifestyle. This way of thinking gave the Beatles an artistic edge that was virtually untouched by their peers.

Going Quantum
"I didn't know what I would find there ..."
("Got to Get You into My Life," 1966)

The progression from the formula of two guitars, bass, and drums on "She Loves You" to the virtuoso musical collage that is *Sgt. Pepper* is breathtakingly swift. After their first few recordings, the Beatles made quantum leaps from album to album.

This kind of leap didn't just happen. It required a conscious desire to evolve. "The first gimmick was the harmonica," said John on the subject. "We started using it on 'Love Me Do' for arrangements, and then we stuck it on 'Please Please Me,' and then on 'From Me to You.' But we dropped it; it got embarrassing to us." In place of gimmicks came attention to artistry.

Much has been made of the Beatles' drug use during their post-Beatlemania period, and this book is not one to condone illicit or illegal drug-taking. However, a close look at fab philosophy shows that experimenting with drugs was not a mere wanton, wasteful lifestyle choice. It was a catalyst of Beatle creativity.

The group never went to the point of no return on using mind-altering substances. There was never a near-fatal overdose. In an interview about his own experimentation with LSD, which in the mid-'60s was a legal medication, Paul explained why: "I was frightened of those things, John was excited, but I was frightened." George was clear on the subject: "It's good to boogie once in a while, but when you boogie all the time, it's just a waste of a life and of what we've been given."

John agreed: "The first effects of the drug [taking] wear off. If you've been in the drug scene, you know it's not something you can go on and on doing. It's like drink [alcohol], you've got to come to terms with it, just like with too much food, you've got to get out of it. You're left with yourself. You've got to get down to your own God, or your own temple in your head."

Nevertheless, without this careful experimentation with drugs, the world would never have known such brilliant musical works as *Sgt. Pepper's Lonely Hearts Club Band*, *Magical Mystery Tour*, and perhaps even the earlier classic *Revolver*, which many critics think are three of the best rock recordings in history.

Mystical writings also figured predominately in Beatle creativity. Here's John discussing "Tomorrow Never Knows": "That's me in my *Tibetan Book of the Dead* period. I took one of Ringo's malapropisms as the title, to take the edge off the heavy philosophical lyrics." Indeed, John was undoubtedly tripping, but this time it was on books by Timothy Leary, Richard Alpert (Ram Dass), and Aldous Huxley. Later, one of the biggest influences on *Sgt. Pepper* was John's favorite writer, Lewis Carroll, author of *Alice's Adventures in Wonderland.* John has said that the hallucinatory imagery in his "Lucy in the Sky with Diamonds" was inspired by Carroll's *Through the Looking-Glass,* where Alice is taken down a river in a boat. "Half of what I say is meaningless," in John's song "Julia," is taken from a phrase in Kahil Gibran's classic, *The Prophet.*

This evolution was also present with all the Beatles' lyrics. From the formulaic "you, me, love" themes early on, the group gravitated toward unconventional subjects such as paperback writers and lonely old spinsters, finally exploding in the sound pictures on *Sgt. Pepper* with "Lucy in the Sky with Diamonds" and "Lovely Rita," about a parking-meter reader.

"One moment I remember," said Paul, "was when we got to that little bit 'I'd love to turn you on' [on 'A Day in the Life'], and John and I looked at each other and thought, 'We're actually saying for the first time ever words like "turn you on"!' There was a little look of recognition that said, 'Do it do it! Get it down!'" It's obvious they were working to bring their ongoing personal, mind-expanding evolution to the world at large.

One last important note, in keeping with the principles of being fab, is that the Beatles were often experimental—sometimes even wildly so—but they always kept their music and presentation accessible, melodic, polished, elegant.

This book is not about encouraging you to take drugs—legal, illegal, under-the-counter, or over-the-counter. But you surely can imagine how a truly *open* mind could open doors in your life—literally. Sure, you'll get guff from your immediate friends and family who've grown used to your patterns, but come on! Shake it up a bit! Think *different*! Your local library has hundreds of books and videotapes on art, spirituality, and philosophy. Why not browse through the works of Picasso, Krishnamurti, and Plato, for example, and study further the works that engage you.

Going Forward

"You say you want a revolution..."
("Revolution," 1968)

Let's take a closer look at the Fabs' studio artistry and their willingness to evolve artistically. With *Sgt. Pepper*, for example, every convention of recording, presenting, and packaging a pop album was challenged in one four-month period. This was not surprising since the group brought an adventurous spirit to their music right at the start. For instance, "She Loves You" ends with the last "yeah!" as a sixth chord influenced by jazz vocal groups such as the Andrews Sisters. Bringing that sort of alternative influence into rock 'n' roll had never been explored previously. The group didn't stop there. They continually offered up many firsts:

★ First record with feedback: "I Feel Fine"
★ First song to begin with a fade-in: "Eight Days a Week"
★ First song to end with a different section other than a chorus: "Ticket to Ride"
★ First pop song backed by a string quartet: "Yesterday"
★ First record with backwards guitar: "I'm Only Sleeping" (achieved manually on the guitar)
★ First record with backwards instrumentation: "Rain" (achieved by running tapes backward)

The Fabs were practicing their evolution philosophy all the way back in August 1965, smack dab in the middle of Beatlemania:

Paul: "We try and change every record. You know, we've tried to change from the first record we made."

George: "And if you progress musically, then you naturally change."

John: "If you play our early records and the newer ones, even though we haven't made all that many, there's a lot of difference."

Getting to "change" took sheer forcefulness and a willingness to lead, not merely to follow the old rules of the technicians and executives at EMI and its corporate-owned Abbey Road studios.

Paul talked about how the group had to push the EMI engineers on every rule in their book. He cited one example [for the song "Nowhere Man"]: "I remember we wanted very treble-y guitars, and the engineer said, 'Alright, I'll put full treble on it,' and we said, 'That's not enough!' He said, 'But that's all I've got.' And we replied, 'Well, put that through another lot of faders and put full treble up on that. And if that's not enough we'll go through another lot of faders.' They said, 'We don't do that!' and we would always say, 'Just try it—if it sounds crappy we'll lose it, but it might just sound good!' You'd then find, 'Oh it worked,' and they'd be secretly glad, because they'd been the engineer who put three times the 'allowed' value of treble on a song. I think they were quietly proud of those things."

This innovation and willingness to consciously evolve as artists took place in a rather antiquated studio at Abbey Road. The first album, *Please Please Me*, was recorded on a mere two tracks, a far cry from today's multitrack computerized studios. These two tracks offered literally no room for overdubs after the fact, meaning that the group had to perform their parts perfectly on the same take or do the entire song over again, which could have proved disastrous on the one day booked for recording a complete album.

George Martin explained how working against studio limitations actually worked to the group's advantage, both in recording and performing: "Producers today would be horrified at [our] restrictions, they're used to recording every sound on its own track." He added, "But because of the 'good-housekeeping' requirement, Paul would be aware that if he made a mistake with his bass playing, he might be ruining a great take from Ringo; and Ringo would be thinking the same thing about his own performance. It was an added spur for them to play well."

In an interview on how they produced *Sgt. Pepper* under trying conditions, George Martin noted, "We were still working on four-track, sometimes linking two machines. We got round the limitations through subterfuge and ingenuity." This shoestring ethos astonished their better-equipped U.S. counterparts. Tommy James, a hit artist and producer, said later he recalled whole studios being torn apart and put back together in search of a single drum sound the Beatles used that American technicians couldn't emulate. He said of the Beatles, "What they did, everything they did, became state-of-the-art."

Innovation is key to being fab! Go with that for a few minutes. Have you gotten into a routine, a grind, even—ouch!—a boring lifestyle? Can being brave and daring in thought and action affect your immediate day-to-day existence? Think about how innovation could affect a project you're working on for your company. Rather than following typical industry trends and copying them, how could a unique new methodology make the project more compelling? The Beatles didn't stand still rewriting big hits like "I Want to Hold Your Hand." They moved on quickly, trying new ideas, constantly pushing the envelope.

Promote Yourself

"I wanna be famous, a star of the screen…"
("Drive My Car," 1965)

The Beatles have long been acknowledged by the MTV network as responsible for the video industry today. Starting with the movies

A *Hard Day's Night* and *Help!*, which featured Beatle songs playing over surrealistic footage, the group quickly moved to producing their own promotional film clips of their newest songs. First came "We Can Work It Out" and "Day Tripper," in December 1965. These first clips were pretty straightforward, but the group evolved. Later films presented an actual *feeling* of the music being played by using surrealistic visual imagery. The clips created for "Strawberry Fields Forever" and "Penny Lane" are excellent examples.

The Fabs were also the first to provide "interview with the artist" audio clips to radio stations, beginning at the time of their first movie. These open-ended interviews were created so that once the initial interview with the Beatles was recorded, the original questions were edited out. Then a local deejay could read scripted questions in synch with the recording, which gave listeners the perception that the Beatles were being personally interviewed by the local deejay.

The Fabs also predated MTV's popular *Unplugged* series, which features top artists—including Paul McCartney—playing songs acoustically with minimum percussion and amplification. In regard to the *Let It Be* album, Paul noted, "I had a copy of the final mixes that [recording engineer] Glyn Johns had done. Today it would sound like MTV's *Unplugged* because it was very basic, very bare. And I thought, 'This is good—really good. We're reduced to just bare bones. There's something great about it. Something very compelling.'" These tapes were later "over-produced" (according to Paul) with overdubs of large choruses and orchestras by producer Phil Spector, in one of the very rare moments the group did not completely control an artistic or business decision.

It's important to note how the group is affecting the world even today in cyberspace. In November 1999, Paul McCartney set a world record with *fifty million* "hits" over the Internet when he performed a concert at the Beatles old incubator, the Cavern Club in Liverpool. And for Paul's first on-line "chat," he drew *three million* questions submitted by e-mail to the event's producer Yahoo!, though the firm was only prepared to use *ten* questions!

Paul was asked in an interview about his Internet interests: "Who designs the MPL Communications site [Paul's publishing company's Web site]? Are you involved?" He replied, "The guys in my office put it together, but I'm pretty hands-on with it. I see it all before anything goes out, and we work out together what goes on it. As I say, I like it to be *right.*" Ditto George. The vision for his Web site for the re-release of George's classic solo album *All Things Must Pass* was dictated directly by him to a team of artists who created a humorous and informative multimedia event according to his specifications.

Maybe the Internet is not part of your promotional plan. But surely, being creative in this department is an important factor of fab wisdom. Famed self-help author Wayne Dyer often recounts his own story of self-promotion during the time of his first book, *Your Erroneous Zones*. Rather than waiting for the publisher to coordinate a book-signing tour or for television and radio programs to call him to be a guest, Wayne took several months off from his job as a college professor, loaded up his station wagon with copies of his books, and drove around the country, drumming up interest. He would literally give books to small New Age shops and beat down the doors of local radio and television shows, finally crystallizing a grassroots word-of-mouth excitement around his book. It paid off. *Your Erroneous Zones* went on to be one of the pioneer books in the self-help genre.

No Such Thing as a Mistake
"It's getting better all the time..."
("Getting Better," 1967)

Ready for this next "being fab" method? How 'bout this? If you make a mistake, you haven't actually *made* a mistake.

Plenty went wrong for the Beatles, but whatever went wrong was immediately canceled out by the group's making the best of it and ultimately turning it right. Let's look at the biggest so-called mistake of the Beatles' career—their decision to personally write and direct the film *Magical Mystery Tour*. The movie, which they had worked on for months and which relied heavily on the wild psychedelic colors of the day, was finally broadcast on television in the then-standard black-and-white. Paul was correct in saying to the press directly after a full-scale critical bashing of the movie, "We could've put on a [typical] 'moptop' show, but we really don't like that sort of entertainment anymore." He added, "We could have sung carols and done a first-class Christmas-y show with lots of phony tinsel like everybody else. That would have been the easiest thing in the world, but we wanted to do something different. If you watch it a second time, it grows on you. That often happens with our records too."

So it does. The adventurous but oft-misunderstood art film has influenced directors like Steven Spielberg. The movie also featured a superb Beatle music soundtrack, including the songs and videos "I Am the Walrus," "Fool on the Hill," and "Blue Jay Way."

On the heels of that film came the animated classic *Yellow Submarine*, which was considered by critics to be a major Beatle mistake even before it went into production. Most thought that successful animated films could only come out of Disney studios, which was the only company producing hit animated movies at the time.

But as any parent knows, even decades after the original *Yellow Submarine* debut, the psychedelic imagery and unique story line has proven enormously successful—artistically and financially. New generations of children have been brought up on it and love it. In fact, to this day, Ringo still gets questions from young kids on why his animated character "pushed the button" that sent his cartoon likeness hurtling through the dangerous sea in the movie.

Indeed, the director and co-writer of Disney's *Toy Story*, John Lasseter, and *Simpsons* creator Matt Groening both cite *Yellow Submarine* as inspirational in their decision to become animators. Finally, *Yellow Submarine* is utilized as the central theme for a popular virtual-reality family-fun ride at a Berlin entertainment center.

Another mistake, which many call the biggest Beatles creative disaster, was the film *Let It Be*. Critics, and even some of the Beatles, cite the film as a bird's-eye view of the disintegration of the bond between four friends. However, those who worked on the film claim that the negative myth tells only half the story. They insist that many scenes which wound up on the cutting-room floor revealed a tone that is lighter, often frivolous, and overall much less bleak.

"I'm sure that's probably quite true," said Paul of the more positive revelations about *Let It Be*, "but what it became was the documentary of a breakup rather than anything else. Those were the most riveting filmic bits, where we're going at each other. I suppose as a director you have to go with that, you just can't start saying, 'Let's make it look pretty.'"

Glyn Johns, George Martin's assistant, is adamant that *Let It Be* was actually "a lot of fun to make" and not the grueling unhappy scene reported about in the press. "I was there when it was being shot," said Glyn, "and there was some amazing stuff. The Beatles' humor got to me as much as the music, and I didn't stop laughing for six weeks! John Lennon only had to walk in a room and I'd just crack up!" He noted further, "Their whole mood was wonderful, that was the thing. There was all this nonsense going on at the time about the problems surrounding the group, and the press being at them. In fact, there they were, just doing it, and having a wonderful time, being incredibly funny. *None of that is in the film!*"

Making mistakes can cripple a life. How often do you reflect on the so-called "mistakes" you've made? Think of "mistakes" as little ankle weights like the ones athletes use. They make a workout more difficult, but they ultimately make you stronger. For the Beatles, the word "mistake" was meaningless. It wasn't in their vocabulary. For the Beatles, some decisions they made during the '60s were considered by their critics to be mistakes. However, in retrospect, *Magical Mystery Tour* and *Let It Be* are today considered to be some of the most innovative and interesting elements of their career. Walking confidently on your journey and using utter intuitive *knowingness* will mean that you'll never ever *ever* make a "mistake."

Breaking New Ground

"I'm fixing a hole where the rain gets in ..."
("Fixing a Hole," 1967)

An enormous amount has been written about other so-called "mistakes" in Beatle business, especially in merchandising and publishing. Some analysts cite that an estimated $50 to $100 million fell through the cracks in merchandising alone during 1963 to 1965. The observers place the blame squarely on the shoulders of manager Brian Epstein. However, on close inspection, Brian made exactly *one single* major blunder during his tenure: his oversight in signing away 90 percent of revenue from Beatle merchandising for such products as dolls, wigs, games, talcum powder, buttons, and all the rest during the height of Beatlemania.

However, we must remember that for the young and fairly inexperienced manager, overwhelmed by the unprecedented success of his "boys," the merchandising marketplace was a completely new and uncharted one, not even considered an industry at that time. Even Elvis Presley, the biggest star in history before the Beatles, never had to deal with this merchandising phenomenon. It simply didn't exist.

And much speculation still arises over how Brian Epstein "badly handled" publishing rights during the early years. For instance, for records sold in North America at three to four dollars apiece, the Beatles received five cents, and in the United Kingdom they earned a single penny per album.

But it's not fair to judge Epstein by the standards of today. The record and publishing deals he and the group signed were standard for the time, long before rock artists had ever heard of such a thing as bargaining power. When the Beatles' popularity took off, it happened on a scale and a speed that was again entirely unprecedented. Epstein worked in a world without signposts. It's doubtful anyone could have served the Beatles better.

Starting the Start-Up
"Would you walk away from a fool and his money?..."
("Come and Get It," 1969)

OK, now we're really at the core of the matter, if you'll excuse the pun, with the establishment of Apple Corps Ltd. in 1968. Begun partly as a way to shelter their collective monies from the British tax laws in effect at the time, Apple was also created as an idealistic dream. Apple was to be a firm that enabled all kinds of artists to produce their work—in records, films, and electronics. John said at the time, "We want to set up a system for people who just want to make a film about anything, and where they don't have to go on their knees in somebody's [corporate] office."

The litany of Apple successes is impressive. "Hey Jude" was the Beatles' first Apple release and went on to become their biggest-selling single at the time. One of the next was "Those Were the Days," which Paul produced, having discovered the song during a visit to a London club in 1965, where he saw the original writer performing it.

Paul also jump-started another Apple group, Badfinger, who were originally signed as the Iveys. One early morning in July, before work on the *Abbey Road* album, Paul played piano, maracas, drums, and bass as well as sang the vocals on a demo for a song he'd written entitled "Come and Get

It." "I always used to get in there early [to Abbey Road studios] because I lived right around the corner," explained Paul. "I ran in and did 'Come and Get It' very quickly, in less than an hour, with the engineer. And I said to the guys in Badfinger, 'You should copy this faithfully.' They said, 'But we'd like to change it a little bit.' I said, 'No, it's absolutely the right arrangement, please don't change this. I can guarantee it's a hit!'"

He was right, and the song went to number one in the United States, effectively launching the group as a hit act that lasted for several years and is still influential in the pop-music industry. In fact, one of the original songs that Badfinger members composed, "Without You," was later a worldwide smash for Harry Nilsson and Mariah Carey.

Apple is now the center of Beatle commerce. *Forbes* magazine consistently lists the Fabs in the top five of entertainment earners, and this is primarily due to the efficiency and organization at Apple. Richard Branson, the U.K.-based billionaire entrepreneur and founder of the Virgin Group (which comprises 150 companies, including Virgin Atlantic Airways), still emulates the concepts behind the early Apple company in his own work. In fact, one of the first controversial acts Branson engaged after founding Virgin Records in the mid-'70s was the Sex Pistols, the groundbreaking punk group who changed the face of rock music. And today, Branson has adopted an extremely successful freewheeling business methodology and personal lifestyle from his initial inspiration from the Fabs' original vision of their Apple Corps.

The Fabs' love of what is now termed "World" music found them working with classical composer John Tavener as early as 1968. After Ringo heard Tavener in concert, he signed the composer to his first recording contract at Apple. And John's main focus at the time was Zapple Records, which produced spoken word and alternative music such as his and Yoko Ono's *Two Virgins* and other avant-garde recordings, which were years ahead of their time.

Now's the time to reflect on that business you've been longing to start. You know who you are! If you've heard a lot of nonsense about how Apple Corps Ltd. was a "hippie-drugged-out money-losing" venture, think again. Apple rocked then, and it still rocks now. Ask Beatle-fan billionaire Richard Branson. At a recent showing of *A Hard Day's Night*, Sir Richard— yes, he was knighted by his home country—was seen "avin' a larf" (wearing a Beatle wig)!

Crisis Management
"I don't really want to stop the show…"
("Sgt. Pepper's Lonely Hearts Club Band," 1967)

In life and in business the unexpected can happen, and often does— sometimes threatening to pull people through emotional turmoil or worse. Let's take a look at several of these out-of-nowhere situations that happened to the Beatles—and what they did about them.

The Beatles continually turned their backs on negative emotions such as fear, disappointment, and resignation, and they met challenges head-on during whatever fiascoes occurred. Let's start with some technical problems during the Fabs' most important live performance ever, the February 1964 *Ed Sullivan Show*.

The tape of the show reveals a clear problem with the live sound to the studio audience, and hence to 73 million viewers. It's for certain that John cannot be heard during "I Want to Hold Your Hand," and it's John's vocal that's the driving lead on the number! True to the fab mind-set, Paul took over on the lead, sacrificing his harmony parts and smiling all the while. The rest of the group, knowing very well what was going on, continued undaunted with John singing into a dead microphone, smiling to the audience. Even more infuriating for the group was the knowledge that they'd taken part in the sound check preceding the show, going as far as adjusting the levels in the sound booth, only to find that just before show-time, someone had rearranged the entire sound board! If there was fear and trepidation at these potentially disastrous technical glitches, the Beatles never showed it during their flawless performance.

Shortly after the outset of Beatlemania, the group came under attack with all sorts of criticism, some of it terrifying. In 1964, for example, the Christian Crusade—a powerful group of religious zealots—warned American parents of what it termed the "Communist Beatle pact." The Christian Crusade distributed flyers and news releases claiming that, through the Beatles, "the Communists have contrived an elaborate, calculating, and scientific technique, directed at rendering a generation of American youth useless through nerve-jarring mental deterioration and retardation." This hatred boiled over in 1966 due to John's off-the-cuff comments about Jesus Christ and England's youth movement to a reporter friend at the *London Evening Standard*: "Christianity will go. It will vanish and shrink. I needn't argue about that. I am right and I will be proved right. We're more popular than Jesus now. I don't know which will go first—rock and roll or Christianity. Jesus was alright, but his disciples were thick and ordinary. It's them twisting it that ruins it for me."

The quote was taken out of context in the United States and reprinted in a glossy teen magazine called *Datebook*. Spread on the cover was the glaring headline, "John Says Beatles Are Bigger Than Jesus!" Reaction in the American South ranged from banning the group's music on radio stations to Ku Klux Klan protests to Beatle-record burnings organized by "Christian" extremists. At the time of all this turmoil, the group was preparing to tour the United States, as they'd done each summer since 1964.

So, what to do if your truly fab? Well, first off, you don't run from the problem. In fact, John earnestly wanted to face the mêlée. He couldn't stand to live with the notion that he'd been responsible for such hate in the world, especially after years of promoting the idea of love in his music.

In Chicago, the first stop of the U.S. tour, John—with the other Beatles standing right behind him—discussed the issue:

Question: "What is your feeling about going down South where most of this controversy has arisen?"
John: "We could have just sort of hidden in England and said, 'Not going, not going!' But straightening it out will be worth it, and good."
Paul: "The thing is, we're just trying to move it in a forward direction. And this is the point, you know. This is why we're getting in all these messes with saying things. Because, you know, we're just trying to *move forward*. And people seem to be trying to just sort of hold us back, and not want us to say anything that's vaguely sort of inflammatory. But I think it's better for everyone if we're just honest about the whole thing."

Paul said it all: Whatever happens—*whatever* happens—*move forward*! This kind of courage, flexibility, and determination *not* to avoid controversy may one day loom in your own dream's future. If so, will you be ready? Examine the worst-case scenarios that could arise as you work to manifest your dreams. Picture them happening and come up with ways you could deal with them. Perhaps you've not given enough thought to possible legal, political, or social ramifications of your dream. What might they be? Fab wisdom says be willing and be ready to handle the toughest situations as they occur.

Keeping a Sense of Humor
"I've got something I can laugh about . . ."
("Good Day Sunshine," 1966)

Humor softened the impact of a multitude of scandals for the Fabs as well. When the "Paul is Dead" rumor began in 1969, the Beatles wisely refused to address it. Their silence caused more clamor and fueled even wilder rumors of an elaborate scheme to hide the fact that Paul had been killed in the mid-'60s. This rumor had its origins as far back as November 1966 after Paul had a moped accident, cutting his upper lip and growing a moustache to cover it.

Some versions of the moped story reported he'd been decapitated, of all things. Fans searched every Beatle album for clues to prove the cover-up was a reality. True to fab form, Paul's eventual humorous comment on the matter quickly put the matter to rest: "I am alive and well, and concerned about the rumors of my death. But if I were dead, I would be the last to know!" Best of all for the Fabs, sales of Beatle albums went through the roof for the months the rumor was rampant.

The Beatles also abated another controversy with a couple of quick but brilliant quips during their so-called Butcher cover scandal. We've already discussed how Capitol Records would put together its own Beatle albums without asking the group's permission or cooperation. By the time Capitol prepared to release another hodgepodge of songs called *'Yesterday' ... and Today* in June 1966—comprised of songs excised from three British versions and sides of earlier 45s—the Beatles would have nothing to do with any of it.

But what was not typical of this newest Capitol release was its startling cover. Instead of the usual photos of four happy smiling moptops, this album's cover offered up the Beatles dressed in butcher smocks, posing with sadistic leers on their faces, adorned with slabs of raw red meat and nude, decapitated dolls.

When disc jockeys who had received advance copies of the album began to complain about its gruesome sleeve, Capitol quickly withdrew the record and reissued it five days later with a substitute cover photograph of the Beatles leaning on a steamer trunk. Many of the 750,000 original butcher cover sleeves went back into record stores with a new cover pasted over the old one. But the Beatles played it smart and said scarcely a word about it. There were no indignant howls of protest from the Beatles, no railing against Capitol Records and its policies. John noted humorously that the cover was "as relevant as Vietnam," and Paul merely chuckled that it was "very tasty meat."

So where did the photo come from? John said later that it was "inspired by our boredom and resentment at having to do another photo session and another Beatles thing. We were all sick to death of it." Australian photographer and artist Roger Whitaker, who took the photos, said, "I had toured quite a lot of the world with them by then, and I was continually amused by the public adulation of four people." To that end, Whitaker planned to form a triptych, something resembling a religious icon, to make the point that the Beatles were just as real and human as everyone else, thereby offering a striking contrast between the Beatle "angelic" image and the reality of the photograph. This appealed to the Fabs' ever-evolving artistry, so they agreed. For instance, one of the unused photos depicts John framing Ringo's head with a cardboard box, and on one of the flaps is written "2,000,000." Whitaker added, "I wanted to illustrate that, in a way, there was nothing more amazing about Ringo than anyone else on this earth. In this life, he was just one of two million members of the human race. The idolization of fans reminded me of the story of the worship of the golden calf."

On July 4, 1966, while on tour in the Philippines, the Beatles were invited to a luncheon by the Marcos family, leaders of the ruling party of the country. Unfortunately, the group never received this invitation, so of course they did not appear. In short order, television and radio coverage cited the group as insulting the country by "refusing to appear" at the function. The Beatles were forced to literally flee Manila without security protection as hundreds of angry Filipinos hurled insults.

After a terrifyingly long wait in their airplane, the group was finally free to leave, but they must have been emotionally shaken. However, films of the Fabs at a press conference directly after arriving back in

London show them calmly discussing the incident, even making jokes about the whole affair. Clearly they were able to put a traumatic episode behind them in a mere matter of hours.

What makes *you* laugh? Certainly, not everyone is naturally funny, but we can all learn from the Beatles way of dealing with problems and frightening situations as they arose. Fab wisdom says to keep a sense of perspective on such issues—and don't sweat over what you can't control.

Seeing the big picture was important for the Fabs. They had long-term goals to realize, so when negative situations came about, they dealt with them in a swift manner and usually with good humor. How equipped are you to deal with problems as they arise? Can you find the humor inherent in sticky situations that come up in your life? Relax! Don't take your dreams so seriously! In the light of all eternity, what does it all mean anyway? Have fun!

YOU'RE THE FIFTH BEATLE! — *Evolution*

★ Check out the more adventurous areas in your chosen profession or avocation. Perhaps you're in the healthcare industry. Instead of just putting the hours in and getting a paycheck, why not begin reading some of the medical journals pertinent to your work? Wouldn't it be exciting to discuss new breakthroughs in the field with your peers? This kind of extracurricular activity could even lead to bigger things for you—a promotion, or speaking engagements, or a raise.

★ The progression from the formula of two guitars, bass, and drums on "She Loves You" to "Tomorrow Never Knows" is fast—less than four years. How can you accomplish this kind of evolution? What will you have to learn? Perhaps you'll need to take night courses to pick up the skills to make that happen—or make a committed effort to locate peers who are working in areas you're interested in.

★ How good are you at working with limitations? For the Beatles, their first album *Please Please Me* was recorded on two tracks—a far cry from today's multitrack studios. How deep is your ability to create an effective and timeless product or service, despite limiting circumstances and equipment? Fab wisdom says to find joy in challenge! Parents know how to transform such limitations as a box of rice and some leftover chicken into a veritable feast. Look through your home. What are some ways of making the most out of antiquated materials around the house or in storage? Maybe that old turntable and collection of classic vinyl rock albums could be the impetus for communication with your teenage kids. Get out those old records, and show your kids the value of the great Motown acts, Dylan, the Stones, and even the Beatles!

★ Are you paralyzed with fear over the possibility of making mistakes— and shutting down your dreams before you get started? For the Beatles, there was *no such thing* as a mistake. They constantly kept their work at a self-imposed level of quality. In doing so, they left virtually no room for the word "mistake" to be held within their vocabulary or in their collective consciousness.

★ How do you fare with crisis management? In front of 73 million viewers, John's microphone cut out. Instead of panicking, Paul immediately took the lead vocal part. The performance went well enough to win over the entire country, taking Beatlemania to new heights. What would you do if at a crucial point in your dream disaster strikes? Complain? Fold up? Or would you do what the Beatles do—be fab!

7 SPIRIT

*All life is worship of God in a way, and all we're doing
is trying to pass it on to more people.
My idea of God is that
you're not doing it for yourself
particularly, but for everyone else.*

—George Harrison

The Beatles have shown us clearly how to live a successful and joyous life, how to manifest our most outrageous and unlimited dreams, and how to do it with inner confidence and a sense of humor about it all. But there's still one more important factor to being fab, one that, if applied, could have a deeply profound effect on your life. Paul said it best, observing that after all the success and all the excess, "There's the next step, you've got to find a *meaning* then."

Throughout this book we've seen glimmers of how much spiritual and social issues meant to the group. The Fabs were not merely four entertainers looking to be *au courant* by chasing the New Age flavor-of-the-moment, nor were they four wealthy people looking for tax write-offs. Rather, after accomplishing every conceivable dream they'd ever had, they began to search for the meaning of it all.

Inviting the Spiritual
"Within You Without You"
(*Sgt. Pepper's Lonely Hearts Club Band*, 1967)

The Beatles' search for spiritual insight was ongoing. "People always got the image I was anti-Christ or anti-religion. I'm not. I'm a most religious fellow," said John. "You don't need the package; you don't need the Christian package or the Marxist package to get the message. I was brought up a Christian, and I only now understand some of the things that Christ was saying in those parables, because people got hooked on the teacher and miss the message."

John discussed the issue of spirituality as early as 1966: "I believe in God, but not as one thing, and not as an 'old man in the sky.' I believe that what people call 'God' is something in all of us. I believe that what Jesus, Muhammad, Buddha, and all the rest said was right." Paul added a few months later, "God is in the space between us. God is in the table in front of you."

Following suit, in the summer of 1966, George took a break from Beatlemania to investigate the possibilities of India. He said at the time, "I went over there partly to try to learn the music, but also to absorb much of the actual country. I'd always heard stories about these masters living in the Himalayas who were hundreds of years old, levitating yogis and saints who could be buried underground for weeks and stay alive. Now I wanted to see it all for myself. I'll tell you one thing for sure, once you get to the point where you're actually doing things for truth's sake, then nobody can ever touch you again, because you're harmonizing with a greater power."

Concurrently, John was studying the mystical *Tibetan Book of the Dead* and used some of the text for his *Revolver* song "Tomorrow Never Knows." This book is the "bible" of Tibetan Buddhism. A concept in Buddhism is of the void and how to reach it. In fact, the working title of John's song was "The Void." George was also busy devouring the *Autobiography of a Yogi*, the life story of Paramahansa Yogananda, the leader of the Self Realization Fellowship and an acclaimed Hindu master who died in the early '60s. At the time, George praised his new influence: "He's probably been the greatest inspiration to me, though I never met Yogananda personally, but he's had such a terrific influence on me for some very subtle reason. A lot of my feelings are the result of what he taught, and is still teaching in his subtle state."

You might be fully satisfied with your own spiritual and religious beliefs. If so—great! But fab wisdom says to investigate all kinds of spiritual systems, along the way discovering new and profound ways to commune with yourself and God. In 1938, Mahatma Gandhi wrote, "There will be no lasting peace on earth unless we learn not merely to tolerate but even to respect the other faiths as our own. A reverent study of the sayings of the different teachers of mankind is a step in the direction of such mutual respect."

The Beatles knew this. Maybe it's time for you to dip into the various sacred texts or even to visit temples, mosques, or churches in your area.

Being Charitable
"Blackbird singing in the dead of night…"
("Blackbird," 1968)

After their experience with the Maharishi in India, the Beatles came back with a fresh new insight into the world's political and social problems. Asked about the poverty in India, Paul noted, "The Maharishi's idea is to stop the poverty at its root. You see, if you just give handouts to people, it will stop the problem for a day or a week. But in India, there are so many people, that you'd need all of America's money poured into India to stop it." He added, "So you've got to get at the cause of it and persuade all the Indians to start doing things, because their religion is very fatalistic. They just sort of sit down and think, 'God said this is the way it is, so it's too bad. We can't do anything about it.' The Maharishi is trying to persuade them that they *can* do something about it."

One of George's first acts after the Beatles' breakup was to hold a massive charity concert for the starvation victims in Bangladesh, which paved the way—years later—for the highly successful "Band-Aid" and "Live-Aid" concerts in the United Kingdom and in the United States. "When I did the Bangladesh concert," said George of the work involved, "I spent a couple of months day and night on the phone trying to trick people into doing it and making a commitment." He added, "Nowadays, it's such an accepted part of life that every so often you give something back to charity."

At a press conference in New York in 1964, the Beatles were asked, "Where would you go in New York City if all this security wasn't necessary?" The immediate answer from all four: "Harlem!" And why not? It was the African American community that had created much of the music they'd grown up listening to. The Beatles were indeed "color-blind" to the talent on those early records and later to the people with whom they toured. They brought Motown artists to the fore during the days of segregation in the United States during the early 1960s.

Motown founder and president Berry Gordy later said of the group, "It helped when we had several songs of ours recorded by the Beatles. I met them and found out that they were great fans of Motown and had been studying Motown music, and they went on to become some of the greatest songwriters in history. We were absolutely delighted at the time." And in their early contracts with promoters in the United States, the Fabs specified in writing that "Artists will not be required to perform before a segregated audience."

Here's Paul at a press conference in 1966 on the subject: "We don't like it if there's any segregation, because we're not used to it, it just seems mad to me. I think it's silly to segregate people, black people are just the same as anyone else. It's stupid. I wouldn't mind them sitting next to *me*, because some of my best friends are black people. There's no segregation of concerts in England, and if there was, we wouldn't play them."

On the subject he chose for his beautiful "Blackbird" in 1968, Paul noted, "I had in my mind a black woman, rather than a bird [British slang for *girl*]. Those were the days of the civil-rights movement, which all of us cared passionately about. So this was really a song from me to a black woman, experiencing these problems in the United States: 'Let me encourage you to keep trying, to keep your faith, there is hope.' As is often the case with my things, a veiling took place. So, rather than say 'black woman living in Little Rock' and be very specific, she became a bird, became symbolic."

This respect for minorities was also evident toward another group that was receiving little if any notice in the mid-'60s. Paul wrote "Lady Madonna" as an homage to the single mother in economic straits who was struggling to keep a job and raise a child at the same time, and this was a decade before the plight of single mothers was discovered by journalists, sociologists, and politicians.

Thirty-five years later, the world is still plagued by social problems such as bigotry, class elitism, and even slavery and teenage prostitution. The message the Beatles gave us all is to love each other. Everyone around us is more important than ever. What specific actions can you take in your own life to make your community a more loving environment to live in? Just writing checks to charity may not be enough. Can you give of yourself and your time? What about the company you work for? Is it doing substantial and effective work to help the community, the state, the country, and the world? Fab wisdom says rise up!

Make Love Not War

"If you go carrying pictures of Chairman Mao…"
("Revolution," 1968)

During the height of the Vietnam War, being fab did not necessarily mean singing protest songs. Others like Bob Dylan and Joan Baez very effectively did that. Instead, the Beatles kept promoting the most timeless answer they knew of—and cared most about—in order to cure the world's ills: *love*.

On occasion, however, they did address the unavoidable topic of war, as in this 1966 press conference:

Question: "What is your opinion of Americans who go to Canada to avoid the draft?"
Paul: "It seems like anyone who feels that fighting is wrong should have the right not to go."
John: "We just don't agree with war. There's no need to kill *anyone*—for *any* reason."
George: "The words 'Thou shalt not kill' mean just that—not 'Amend section A.' There's no reason whatsoever for killing. No one can force you to kill anyone if you feel it's wrong."

For John, extracurricular activities also found him becoming an unrelenting and influential peace activist. Along with partner and lover Yoko Ono, he traversed the world holding "Bed-Ins for Peace" and creating related marketing campaigns such as the famed "War is Over (If You Want It)" promotion. Commercial suicide? The press thought so. John and Yoko were painted as "clowns" and "fools" time and again for their efforts. Films of the Bed-Ins show humorist Al Capp railing on the two activists: "Whatever race you're the representative of, I ain't a part of it!" John didn't care—his passion took precedence.

During a series of Bed-In interviews, John was clear on the subject of the perils of war: "People sit around pointing fingers at Nixon and the leaders of the countries, saying, 'He gave us peace, or he gave us war,' when it's actually *our* responsibility what happens around the world. It's our responsibility for Vietnam, and all the other wars that we don't quite hear about. It's all *our* responsibility, and when we all want peace we'll get it."

John and Yoko's campaign, though at the time portrayed by the media as something of a joke, is now considered by many historians to be an influential factor in the Nixon administration finally calling an end to the Vietnam war in 1972.

It might be difficult to imagine yourself in the role of activist. The thought of it brings to mind self-sacrifice, complete and utter concern for others, and possible negative reaction from those who disagree. But there are ways to participate in social change involving ideas that intrigue you. What issues really push your hot buttons? Child abuse, bigotry, women's salary equality in the workplace, global warming? Make contact with groups in your area that really do something about these problems.

Loving Meditation
"Turn off your mind, / Relax and float downstream..."
("Tomorrow Never Knows," 1966)

One of the most profound and sweeping changes the Beatles prompted in the Western world was spurring interest in the spiritual technique of meditation. Long before Deepak Chopra—himself a student of the Maharishi—and the New Age workshops that dot every small town today, the Maharishi Mahesh Yogi taught transcendental meditation. The Fabs practiced meditation, replacing their chemically induced "highs" with natural and spiritual ones.

With their new love of meditation, the group found the much-needed peace to continue their artistic pace, and they found it within their own minds, or rather, in turning *off* their minds. "Maharishi made a lot of sense, I liked him quite a lot," said Paul. "I think we all did, because with a simple system of meditation, twenty minutes in the morning and twenty minutes in the evening, with no big crazy thing, you could improve the quality of your life, and find some sort of *meaning* in doing so."

The "Come on, come on! Come on is such a joy! Come on is make it easy" lyrics from John's "Everybody's Got Something to Hide Except for

Me and My Monkey" is actually a word-for-word teaching from the Maharishi. Likewise, John's "Across the Universe" includes a mantra at the end, "Jai Guru Deva," a reference to the Maharishi's spiritual teacher, Guru Dev. Guru Dev was the Maharishi's guru/teacher, so "Jai Guru Dev" means literally "I give thanks to Guru Dev (or heavenly teacher)." (*Deva* is the feminine of *Dev.*) Though John did later have a falling out with the guru and even wrote a nasty song about his experience called "Maharishi"—which was later retitled "Sexy Sadie"—he eventually recanted somewhat, saying he was "probably too hard" on the Maharishi.

In fact, Paul still practices transcendental meditation daily. "I still mediate every day for a half-hour in the morning and half-hour every evening, and I think I'm a better person for it. I'm far more relaxed than I have ever been," Paul noted. "If you've been working very hard, and things are a bit chaotic, you get all tensed up and screwed up inside, and you feel as if you have to break something or hit someone. But if you spend a short while in the mornings and evenings meditating, it completely relaxes you, and it's easier to see your way through problems. If everyone in the world started meditating, the world would be a much happier place."

And in the End
"The love you take is equal to the love you make…"
("The End," 1969)

Leaving a legacy of love is a huge part of living your life the Beatles way. While following their dream, the four lads from Liverpool certainly gave the world an enormous amount of joy. Your life, as you pursue your dream and share your talents, is just as capable of leaving a legacy of love.

Regarding the Beatles' recording "All You Need Is Love" on its first worldwide television broadcast in 1967, Paul said, "We had been told we'd be seen recording it by the whole world at the same time. So we had one message for the world: love." And as George noted, "We'll just sing 'All You Need Is Love,' because it's a subtle kind of public relations for God."

In fact, that one word *love* is highlighted in Beatle song titles seventeen times, and of course love is the central theme in most of their songs. The Beatles' first released recording is called "Love Me Do," and their last, on *Anthology*, is "Real Love." "I'm really glad that most of the Beatles' songs dealt with love, peace, and understanding," said Paul. "There was a very good *spirit* behind it all."

John was adamant about this too: "I still believe in the fact that love is what we all need."

Ringo added his view on the subject: "It was for love. I even get excited now, when I realize that's what it was for, people putting flowers in guns. It was exciting times, and all for this loving feeling."

George agreed, at the height of his young success in 1964, when an interviewer asked him what the most important thing is in life. "Love," he answered.

And Paul sets the fab philosophy straight on this subject: "'Love Me Do' was the Beatles' greatest philosophical song." He sings, "Love, love me do, / You know I love you. / I'll always be true."

Paul sums up beautifully and elegantly: "It's simple, and it's *true*."

YOU'RE THE FIFTH BEATLE! —SPIRIT

Here are five ways to help you look within to find your own spiritual muse:

★ Where are you currently with your own religious faith? Fab wisdom says to take more than a cursory interest in spiritual matters. Next time you stop at the library, you might want to take a read on some of the sacred texts of interest to you in your own faith or that of others. And being fab means opening your mind and your heart.

★ The Beatles spoke out publicly about the poverty they saw during their stay in India, when most in the Western world knew little about it. The Beatles also performed at charity shows, even during the Beatlemania days. After an exhausting second tour of the United States in 1964, they performed one last show for the United Cerebral Palsy and Retarded Infants Services—and did not accept a fee. What are *your* feelings about the terrible straits people suffer in much of the rest of the world? Are you willing to work for causes that will benefit those in need? You don't need to go to India to look at poverty. There are plenty of causes to volunteer for right in your local area. How can you help?

★ Like the Beatles, do you have the courage to speak your mind in public about controversial global or local issues? Think of ways that would end world problems, such as John and Yoko's "Bed-Ins for Peace" campaigns. Tune to CNN to see the hopelessness and despair that much of the world is struggling through. What moves your heart? Take a walk in your city. Does your heart break each time you see a homeless person? You might even know of spousal or child abuse going on in your own neighborhood. Take some time to reflect on what you can personally do about these situations. Start small. Fab wisdom means changing the world—first within, then locally, then in your community, and over time, taking your message to the world at large.

★ Investigate techniques like transcendental meditation in order to find a peace within. It might also help to simply stop what you're doing for just a few minutes each day to reflect on your life and your dreams.

★ The Beatles meant it when they sang "All You Need Is Love." In fact, most of their songs centered on the subject of love. Make sure to play at least one love-drenched Beatle song each day—there's plenty to choose from! When you do, take the time to reflect on the awesome power of love and how it can change yourself, the immediate community around you, and even the whole world. We've got some of the greatest role models— the Beatles. Let's all work to make their legacy of love a continuing reality—by living the Beatles way.

If the Beatles had a message,
it was to learn to swim. Period!
And once you learn to swim — swim.

—John Lennon

We began this book with a quote from Paul McCartney: "The Beatles way of life was like a young kid entering the big world, entering it with friends, and conquering it totally." It's only fitting to end this book with the important message above from John.

The seven principles in living life the Beatles way clearly show how those four teens from "Liddypool" were able to conquer the world—not with violence and war but in the name of love, the rarest of achievements.

These fab principles carried over into the four solo careers for John, Paul, George, and Ringo, and in fact, they still drive the three surviving members to ever-higher, ever-exciting dimensions of success, artistry, and joy.

John's solo career, up until his death at age forty, produced a fascinating legacy. He and his partner, Yoko, gave the world some of the best avant-garde music ever recorded. And John continually thrilled the world with hits such as "Whatever Gets You through the Night." His inspirational anthems "Imagine," "Give Peace a Chance," and "War is Over (If You Want It)" still bring hope to millions across the globe.

Additionally, John's final album, *Double Fantasy*, released just weeks prior to his death, while a beautiful testament to family and domestic life, still featured his lifelong love affair with rock 'n' roll.

There's the Paul McCartney who gave us "Silly Love Songs" with his mega-popular group Wings, several sold-out world tours, and a string of hit records which kept him on top of the charts throughout the '70s and '80s. The acclaim of Paul's early film score *The Family Way* from 1966 preceded the more recent classical compositions *Liverpool Oratorio*, *Standing Stone*, and *A Garland for Linda*, for which Paul is winning the respect of his peers and gaining himself a whole new audience. He is also at the forefront of New Age ambient music with his "Fireman" and *Liverpool Sound Collage* recordings.

Paul's acumen as a music publisher is earning him a million dollars per week. In fact, Paul's company, MPL Communications, is the most successful independent music publisher in the world. His love affair with Linda Eastman thrived for thirty years until she passed away in 1998. Paul has continued his fab philanthropy by helping to raise funds needed to refurbish his alma mater, the Liverpool Institute, which now houses the Liverpool Institute of Performing Arts. And Paul continues the activism he publicly displayed with the release of his controversial—and banned— "Give Ireland Back to the Irish" in the early '70s, by continuing his legacy as an animal-rights activist, and by championing myriad social causes he cares passionately about.

We have the George Harrison who gave us "My Sweet Lord" and his own legacy of hit records, along with several years of sold-out tours. George also undertook the breakthrough "Concert for Bangladesh" benefit, which gave the entertainment industry the model now deployed in raising billions for world causes. He's also a successful movie producer and still produces the music he loves, including his continuing work with Ravi Shankar.

And of course, there's the ex-Beatle who wrote and sang "It Don't Come Easy" and several other hits and who also had a successful run as an actor. Today, Ringo Starr entertains tens of thousands of fans with his popular "All-Starr Band" concert tours—ever-flashing his famous two-fingered "peace sign" and never letting us forget that, indeed, love is all we need.

Living the Beatles way means thinking in an unlimited way. It means dreaming and living out those dreams. It means making the world a better place in which to live. It's a place where each of us can freely express ourselves through our own uniquely creative elegance. Along the way, we can spread the power of love to each and every heart throughout the world—now and for generations yet to come.

ACKNOWLEDGMENTS

Like any labor of love, I suppose, this book took many months to write—and a lifetime. As a first-generation Beatles fan, my great obsession these past forty years has not been simply the great music. Rather, it hit me early on just how *cool* the Fab Four were; and later, how adventurous and courageous; and later still, how spiritual they dared to be. One big Beatle moment in my life—among countless such moments—occurred a few years ago when the Hindu teacher I'd been studying with—but whom I had not met—walked into the lecture room: white robe streaming, brown skin gleaming, long gray hair and beard flowing in his wake. He looked *exactly* like the Fabs' guru Maharishi—and I immediately thought, "Yes! Now, I'm officially a *Beatle*!"

I wish to express my gratitude to the people who made my life fab—and this book possible.

To the strongest, most loving, and most spiritually adventurous person I've ever known: my mother, Edith Price Lange. Mom, thanks for playing me "She Loves You" on your 45-rpm record player, for letting me stay up late to watch *Ed Sullivan* the night the Fabs were on, and for taking me to *A Hard Day's Night*. You *knew*. And thanks for taking me to the Jefferson Airplane concert in '68. I *got* it—peace and love is truly the answer.

To Dad. Though you've left this plane, your unconditional love and encouragement was always there for me—and always will be.

To my brother, David, who beat hell. You continue to inspire me with your enthusiasm for life.

To Ramtha and JZ Knight, my teachers who gave me life worth living. To life! And to Greg Simmons, a Master beyond words. Thanks for introducing me to Beyond Words.

To Larry Ether, my best friend, unconditionally.

To Eilene Tarrao. We'll always be partners, no matter what.

To Dale Anderson. You've been my untiring enthusiast, and you never let me forget my worth and potential. I won't let you forget yours.

To John Barilla, love personified. I can't wait to see your own writing dreams, and all your dreams, manifest into realities.

To Steve Erdman. There are not many true geniuses. You are one, and I look forward to the rest of the world discovering that fact.

To Peter Krass. Your quiet brilliance and loving heart impacts everyone around you. Thanks for your belief in me.

To Sean Hawley, Gene Rogers, Rocky Martino, Steve Langevin, Susan Emory, and Lisa Berzolla. Thanks for taking me in. It's my sincerest wish that you each live out every dream you choose to make a reality.

To the beautiful people at Beyond Words. First, to Cindy Black and Richard Cohn. You took an intuitive chance on me, and I humbly thank you. Your work has touched countless thousands, perhaps millions, throughout the world, and your vision of enabling people to live to their utmost is a mission we should all aspire to. Thanks to my awesome editor, Laura Carlsmith. You made this book come alive. Kudos to Joy Collman, Julie Steigerwaldt, Karolyn Nearing, Sylvia Hayes, Dorral Lukas, and Marvin Moore for all your hard work. And a Fab-style "Yeah!" to Greg Tozian. Your initial edit challenged me to make this book superb.

To the Beatles: John, Paul, George, and Ringo. This book is my love letter to you.

BIBLIOGRAPHY

BOOKS AND MAGAZINES

Axlerod, Mitchell. *Beatletoons: The Real Story behind the Cartoon Beatles*. New York: Wynn Publishing, 1999.

Badman, Keith. *The Beatles off the Record: Outrageous Opinions and Unrehearsed Interviews*. London: Omnibus Press, 2000.

Bennahum, David. *The Beatles after the Breakup*. London: Omnibus Press, 1991.

Brown, Peter, and Steven Gaines. *The Love You Make: An Insider's Story of the Beatles*. New York: McGraw-Hill, 1983.

Carr, Roy. *Beatles at the Movies*. New York: HarperPerennial, 1996.

Cleave, Maureen. "How Does a Beatle Live? John Lennon Lives Like This." *London Evening Standard*, March 4, 1966.

Davis, Hunter. *The Beatles*. New York: McGraw-Hill, 1985.

Dean, Johnny, ed. *The Beatles Monthly Book* (London: Parker Mead for Beat Publications), June 2000, p. 45.

Doggett, Peter. *The Beatles: The Summer of 1968*. Edited by Paul Wane. Lancashire, England: Tracks Books, 1995.

Epstein, Brian. *A Cellarful of Noise*. New York: Doubleday, 1964.

Ferguson, Alasdair, and Alf Bicknell. *Ticket to Ride*. London: Glitter Books, 1999.

Fields, Danny. *Linda McCartney: A Portrait*. Los Angeles: Renaissance Books, 2000.

Fulpen, H. V. *The Beatles: An Illustrated Diary*. New York: Perigee Books, 1982.

Gambaccini, Paul. "The Rolling Stone Interview: Paul McCartney." *Rolling Stone*, January 31, 1974, pp. 32–34, 38–46.

Goodman, Joan. "Playboy Interview: Paul and Linda McCartney—Candid Conversation." *Playboy*, December 1984, pp. 75–110.

Greenwald, Ted. *The Long and Winding Road: An Ultimate Guide to the Beatles*. New York: Friedman/Fairfax Publishers, 1995.

Harrison, George. *I Me Mine*. New York: Simon & Schuster, 1980.

Hertsgaard, Mark. *A Day in the Life: The Music and Artistry of the Beatles*. New York: Delacorte Press, 1995.

Lennon, John. *In His Own Write*. New York: Buccaneer Books, 1964.

Lewinsohn, Lewis. *The Beatles Recording Sessions*. New York: Harmony Books, Crowne Books, 1988.

————. *The Complete Beatles Chronicle*. London: Octopus Publishing Group Ltd., Pyramid Books, 1992.

MacDonald, Ian. *Revolution in the Head: The Beatles' Records and the Sixties*. New York: Henry Holt, 1994.

Martin, George, and William Pearson. *With a Little Help from My Friends: The Making of Sgt. Pepper*. Boston: Little, Brown, 1994.

McCartney, Mike. *The Macs: Mike McCartney's Family Album*. New York: Putnam Books, Delilah Books, 1981.

Meryman, Richard. "Paul McCartney on the Beatle Breakup," *Life* magazine, April 16, 1971, pp. 52–58.

Miles, Barry. *The Beatles: A Diary*. New York: Omnibus Press, 1998.

————. *Paul McCartney: Many Years from Now*. New York: Henry Holt, 1997.

Norman, Phillip. *Shout: The Beatles in Their Generation*. New York: Simon & Schuster, Fireside Books, 1981.

Pemberton, Andy, ed. "The Beatles: Band of the Century." *Q* magazine (London), December 1999.

Rayl, A. J. S., and Curt Gunther. *Beatles '64: A Hard Day's Night in America*. New York: Doubleday, 1989.

Sandison, David. *The Beatles: 1969–70*. London: UFO Music Ltd.,1996.

Sheff, David. "Playboy Interview: John Lennon and Yoko Ono—Candid Conversation." *Playboy*, January 1981, pp. 75–114, 144.

Shepherd, Jean. "Playboy Interview: The Beatles—Candid Conversation." *Playboy*, February 1965, pp. 51–60.

Solt, Andrew, and Sam Egan. *Imagine: John Lennon*. New York: Macmillan, Sarah Lazin Books, 1988.

Spencer, Terence. *It Was Thirty Years Ago Today*. London: Bloomsbury Publishing Ltd., 1995.

Spizer, Bruce, and Alan W. Livingston. *The Beatles' Story on Capitol Records*. New Orleans, La.: 498 Production, L.L.C., 2000.

Taylor, Derek. *As Time Goes By*. London: Davis-Poynter, 1973.

————. *It Was Twenty Years Ago Today*. New York: Simon & Schuster, Fireside Books, 1987.

Turner, Steve. *A Hard Day's Write: The Story behind Every Beatles Song*. New York: HarperCollins, 1999.

Wenner, Jann. *Lennon Remembers*. New York: Popular Library, 1971.

————. "The Rolling Stone Interview: John Lennon." Parts 1 and 2. *Rolling Stone*, January 21, 1971, pp. 32–35, 37–42; February 4, 1971, pp. 36–43.

INTERVIEW CDS

Beatles Tapes II. Jerden, 1995.

The Beatles: Quote Unquote. MagMid (TKO Magnum Music), 1995.

Giuliano, Geoffrey, and Glenn A. Baker. *The Beatles Inside Interviews*. Delta Music, 1995.

Greisman, Michael, producer. *The Beatles: West Coast Invasion*. Cicadelic Records, 1993.

Greisman, Michael, producer. *Not a Second Time*. TKO Music Ltd, 2000.

Kane, Larry. *The Fab Four on Tour*. The Wall, 1996.

The Legends Collection: The John Lennon Collection. Dressed to Kill, 2000.

Steck, Jim, and Dave Hull. *Hear the Beatles Tell All*. Charly Holdings, 1994.

VIDEOS AND BROADCASTS

Alf Bicknell's Personal Beatles Diary. Jack Edwards Productions (Simitar Entertainment), 1996.

The Beatles: Anthology. Apple Corps Ltd., London, 1996.

The Beatles: The First U.S. Visit. Apple Corps Ltd., London, 1990.

The Beatles: The Legend Continues. Simitar Entertainment, 1991.

The Beatles Story: Days of Beatlemania. White Star (Kultur), 1991.

The Beatles Unauthorized. MerseySound and GoodTimes Video Productions, 1996.

The Compleat Beatles. Delilah Films (MGM/UA Home Video Inc.), 1988.

The Magical Mystery Trip. Vex Films, ArtRock, and Philip Cushway, 1992.

The Making of "A Hard Days Night." MPI Home Video, 1995.

The Making of Sgt. Pepper. A Really Useful Group, 1992.

So Far Out It's Straight Down (interview with Paul McCartney), BBC, March 7, 1967 (transcript: *http://www.geocities.com/~beatleboy1/dbpm.67.html*).

WORLD WIDE WEB SITES

All About the Beatles Butcher Cover:
http://www.eskimo.com/~bpentium/butcher.html

Beathoven.com: *http://www.beathoven.com*

Beatle Links.net: Your Beatles Internet Resource Guide:
http://www.beatlelinks.net/links

The Beatles at the Web Spot: *http://www.harddaysnight.org*

Beatles Beatles Beatles (Pepperland):
http://members.tripod.com/~taz4158/pepper.html

The Beatles Chronicle in Vinyl:
http://www.geocities.com/SunsetStrip/Auditorium/1170/Contents.html

Beatles' Lost Gig: *http://www.beatles-thelostgig.com*

Beatle Money: *http://www.fortunecity.com/tinpan/manicstreet/526*

Beatles News Briefs: *http://www.geocities.com/abbeyrdwebmaster*

Beatles Related Articles:
http://www.geocities.com/CapitolHill/Lobby/7049/index.html#beatles

The Beatles Ultimate Experience: *http://www.geocities.com/~beatleboy1*

The Beatles Ultimate Resources:
   http://www.fortunecity.com/tinpan/ash/618/main2.htm
BeatleZone: *http://www.beatlezone.com/bz.news.html*
Blacklisted Journalist. "The Beatles' Triumphant Return to Liverpool":
   http://www.bigmagic.com/pages/blackj
Internet Beatles Album: *http://www.getback.org/bmain.html*
Leaf, David. "Interview with Paul McCartney on Pet Sounds" (1990):
   http://www.brianwilson.com
Leaf, David. "The Beach Boys: The Pet Sounds Sessions" (1994):
   http://www.brianwilson.com
Meet the Beatles: *http://members.tripod.com/~holysm0ke/index.html*
Off the Beatle Track: The Website of the Beatles London News and
   Information Service: *http://www.beatlesnews.com*

OTHER BOOKS FROM
BEYOND WORDS PUBLISHING, INC.

So, You Wanna Be a Rock Star?
How to Create Music, Get Gigs, and Maybe Even Make It Big!
Author: Stephen Anderson; Illustrator: Zachary Snyder
$8.95, softcover

So, You Wanna Be a Rock Star? is a hip, how-to book that teaches young aspiring musicians how to achieve their rock-and-roll dreams. The book contains both practical advice and cool insights into how real bands got discovered. In a fun and informative style, author Stephen Anderson tells kids how they can start their own band with their friends, a set of drums, and a lot of inspiration.

Taming Your Inner Brat
A Guide for Transforming Self-Defeating Behavior
Author: Pauline Wallin, Ph.D.
$14.95, softcover

An inner brat?!! Who, me?? We've all got one: that force within us which compels us to sneak just one more cigarette or cookie, procrastinate on taxes, or throw a hissy fit when the store clerk takes too long. With humor and without scolding, *Taming Your Inner Brat* gives readers specific strategies and skills to bring bratty thoughts, feelings, and behaviors under control. The author explains the psychological sources of the inner brat and addresses social and cultural conditions that encourage the self-centeredness and sense of entitlement on which the inner brat thrives. By teaching us how to recognize our inner brat, *Taming Your Inner Brat* helps us bring problems into manageable perspective and make changes that last.

Watermelon Magic
Seeds of Wisdom, Slices of Life
Author: Wally Amos, $14.95 softcover

Watermelon Magic is an inspirational/motivational book using watermelons as a metaphor for life. Utilizing the life experiences of Wally Amos, the book shows the parallels between watermelons and humans. *Watermelon Magic* tells how Wally Amos uses his faith in everyday life and the wisdom gained from the past to help him make wise choices. Just as the vine connects the watermelons, we are all connected by spirit. And just as prickly vines make it difficult to get the melons, our human connections are sometimes prickly, making it difficult for us to achieve our goals and realize our dreams. *Watermelon Magic* helps us acknowledge the difficulties and choose a path to success.

The Intuitive Way

A Guide to Living from Inner Wisdom
Author: Penney Peirce; Foreword: Carol Adrienne
$16.95, softcover

When intuition is in full bloom, life takes on a magical, effortless quality; your world is suddenly full of synchronicities, creative insights, and abundant knowledge just for the asking. *The Intuitive Way* shows you how to enter that state of perceptual aliveness and integrate it into daily life to achieve greater natural flow through an easy-to-understand, ten-step course. Author Penney Peirce synthesizes teachings from psychology, East-West philosophy, religion, metaphysics, and business. In simple and direct language, Peirce describes the intuitive process as a new way of life and demonstrates many practical applications from speeding decision-making to expanding personal growth. Whether you're just beginning to search for a richer, fuller life experience or are looking for more subtle, sophisticated insights about your spiritual path, *The Intuitive Way* will be your companion as you progress through the stages of intuition development.

Nurturing Your Child with Music

How Sound Awareness Creates Happy, Smart, and Confident Children
Author: John M. Ortiz, Ph.D.
$14.95, softcover

Author and psychomusicologist Dr. John Ortiz says that we have "just begun to tap into the powers behind the timeless element of sound," and in his book *Nurturing Your Child with Music*, Dr. Ortiz allows the readers to discover those musical powers through and with their children. Designed for parents who take an active interest in their children's lives, this book offers a number of creative methods through which families can initiate, enhance, and maintain happy, relaxed, and productive home environments. *Nurturing Your Child with Music* includes easy-to-do exercises and fun activities to bring music and sound into parenting styles and family life. The book provides music menus and sample "days of sound" to use during the prenatal, newborn, preschool, and school-age phases. Dr. Ortiz shares how we can keep our family "in tune" and create harmony in our homes by inviting music and sound into our daily dance of life.

PowerHunch!

Living an Intuitive Life
Author: Marcia Emery, Ph.D.; Foreword: Leland Kaiser, Ph.D.
$15.95, softcover

Whether it's relationships, career, balance and healing, or simple everyday decision-making, intuition gives everyone an edge. In *PowerHunch!* Dr. Emery is your personal trainer as you develop your intuitive muscle. She shows you how to consistently and accurately apply your hunches to any problem and offers countless examples of intuition in action, covering a wide spectrum of occupations and relationships. With its intriguing stories and expert advice, *PowerHunch!* gives you the necessary tools and principles to create an intuitive life for yourself.

Hindsights

The Wisdom and Breakthroughs of Remarkable People
Author: Guy Kawasaki
$22.95, hardcover

What have you learned from your life that you would like to share with the next generation? Get a fresh appreciation of the human experience in this inspirational collection of interviews with thirty-three people who have overcome unique challenges. They are candid about their failures and disappointments, and insightful about turning adversity into opportunity. Guy Kawasaki spent over two years researching and interviewing such people as Apple Computer co-founder Steve Wozniak, management guru Tom Peters, and entrepreneur Mary Kay. But not everyone in the book is a celebrity. They share their revelations and life experiences, motivating the reader for both personal and professional growth.

To order or to request a catalog, contact
Beyond Words Publishing, Inc.
20827 N.W. Cornell Road, Suite 500
Hillsboro, OR 97124-9808
503-531-8700 or 1-800-284-9673

You can also visit our Web site at *www.beyondword.com*
or e-mail us at *info@beyondword.com*.

BEYOND WORDS PUBLISHING, INC.

OUR CORPORATE MISSION
Inspire to Integrity

OUR DECLARED VALUES
We give to all of life as life has given us.

We honor all relationships.

Trust and stewardship are integral to fulfilling dreams.

Collaboration is essential to create miracles.

Creativity and aesthetics nourish the soul.

Unlimited thinking is fundamental.

Living your passion is vital.

Joy and humor open our hearts to growth.

It is important to remind ourselves of love.